CRICKET

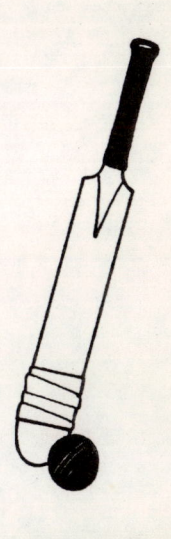

CRICKET QUIZ BOOK

CRICKET QUIZ BOOK

Hugh Larkin and Gareth Wells

Tynron Press, Scotland

© *Hugh Larkin and Gareth Wells, 1992*

First published in 1992 by
Tynron Press
Stenhouse
Thornhill
Dumfriesshire DG3 4LD
Scotland

ISBN 1-85646-019-3
All rights reserved

Cover and illustrations by Lee Nicholls
Typeset by Linographic Services Pte Ltd
Printed in Singapore by General Printing Services Pte Ltd

CONTENTS

SECTION I — TESTS 1

The Ashes, South Africa, West Indies, New Zealand, India, Pakistan, Sri Lanka, Test Caps, One-cap Men, Youngest and Oldest, Test Captains, Answers

SECTION II — FEATS 27

Batting Disasters, Boundaries, Catches Win Matches, Close Ones, Ducks, Fielders, Hat Tricks, Plus "50" Averages, Run-outs, Thousand Runs Plus, The "400" Men, Wicketkeepers, Answers

SECTION III — THE COUNTIES 47

Derbyshire, Essex, Glamorgan, Gloucestershire, Hampshire, Kent, Lancashire, Leicestershire, Middlesex, Northamptonshire, Nottinghamshire, Somerset, Surrey, Sussex, Warwickshire, Worcestershire, Yorkshire, Answers

SECTION IV — THE COUNTY SCENE 83

Around Britain, Badges, Colours And Ties, Lord's, Overseas Visitors, Transfers, Umpires, Who Did They Play For?, Answers

SECTION V — THE TROPHIES 95

The World Cup, The Prizes, Benson and Hedges Cup, Early Championships, Gillette Cup/NatWest Trophy, Sunday League, Winners Around The World, Answers

SECTION VI — GREAT PLAYERS 111

Sir Donald Bradman, Denis Compton, Ian Botham, Geoff Boycott, Richie Benaud, Sydney S.F. Barnes, Bhagwant Chandrasekher, Sir Learie Constantine, Greg Chappell, Kapil Dev, Sunil Gavaskar, W.G. Grace, David Gower, Lance Gibbs, Clarrie Grimmett, Patsy Hendren, Sir Jack Hobbs, Sir Len Hutton, Michael Holding, Sir Richard Hadlee, Walter Hammond, Imran Khan, Jim Laker, Ray Lindwall, Dennis Lillee, Clive Lloyd, "Vinoo" Mankad, Mushtaq Mohammed, Keith Miller, Javed Miandad, Mike Proctor, Barry Richards, Viv Richards, Wilfred Rhodes, Sir Garfield Sobers, Zaheer Abbas, Frank Woolley, Gundappa Vishwanath, Glenn Turner, Bill Pansford, Sir Frank Worrell, Everton Wakes, Doug Walters, Rodney Marsh, John Snow, Derek Underwood, F.E. Spofforth, Fred Trueman, Graeme Pollock, Gordon Greenidge, Answers

SECTION VII — A MIXED BAG

Aristocracy, Bodyline, Commentators, Double-barrellers, Families, Grounds, Initials, League Cricket, Minor Counties, Nicknames, Oddities, Two Sports, Unusual Dismissals, Odd One Out, Oxford V. Cambridge, Rest Of The World, Scratch Teams, Twelve To Find, Women's Cricket, Answers

SECTION I
TESTS

1	The Ashes	2
2	South Africa	4
3	West Indies	5
4	New Zealand	6
5	India	8
6	Pakistan	9
7	Sri Lanka	10
8	Test Caps	11
9	One-cap Men	13
10	Youngest And Oldest	13
11	Test Captains	14
12	Answers	17

TESTS

Not unexpectedly, we commence our sojourn among the questions at the zenith of the game. Questions on the Test-playing nations, the Ashes and some of the star performers.

THE ASHES

The most famous Test rubber of all.

1) Who was the first man to register a "ton" in the England-Australia Tests? And in which year?

2) Who skippered the following Australian touring sides?
   i) 1934   iii) 1964
   ii) 1953   iv) 1981

3) How many Tests were there, in each of the ensuing lists of series?
   i) 1938   iii) 1979-80
   ii) 1975   iv) 1985

4) What are the respective best series results for each nation?

5) Hutton and Bradman have posted the highest individual innings for their countries but which players possess the respective second bests? And when were they achieved?

6) Which bowler turned in the top-notch analysis by an Australian?

7) On how many occasions did the following post a ten-wicket Ashes Test?
   i) Harold Larwood
   ii) Fred Trueman
   iii) Dennis Lillee
   iv) Rodney Hogg

8) Who are the respective combatant's leading centurions?

9) What are the highest fourth innings totals that have been registered?
   i) To win   ii) Lose

10) Which two batsmen share the record partnership for any Ashes wicket? What score was it? When was it completed?

11) When was the last occurrence of the carrying of a bat in an Ashes rubber?

12) An Australian is the top wicket-taker in a series? Who and when?

13) Which pair were responsible for an English sixth wicket stand of 215 in 1977?

14) Jim Laker's "ten" is England's best but who registered the Aussie innings record?

Cricket Quiz Book

15) Who was the last batsman who struck a "ton" in what was both his Test and Ashes debut?

SOUTH AFRICA

South Africa were the next nation to enter the lists in Test cricket.

1) The Ashes pair were joined by South Africa in which year?

2) What was the result of the last completed rubber between England and South Africa?

3) Only one bowler has recorded nine wickets in a Test innings for the Springboks. Name him.

4) South Africa's record Test knock was the work of who, and how many did he labour for?

5) Whose 545-minute century stood for 20 years as the most painstaking effort of its kind?

6) Two Springboks scored a hundred in each innings of a Test in a 1947 series. Name them.

7) Graeme Pollock maintained a phenomenal average over his Test career. In round figures what was it?

Tests

8) A South African "stumper" has removed six batsmen in an innings, eight in a Test and 24 in a series. Who has this remarkably impressive set of personal bests?

9) Only one Springbok reached the Test "double" (1,000 runs/100 wickets or more). Name the player.

10) Which South African notched the only "Bok" double-ton against England? And with a broken thumb as well!

WEST INDIES

The Caribbean Islands entered the fray for the first time in 1928.

1) Who is the only batsman ever to score a hundred and double-hundred in his first Test match?

2) How many West Indies batsmen have topped 250 in a Test innings?

3) Who is the sole West Indian to take nine wickets in a Test innings?

4) Michael Holding, Joel Garner, Malcolm Marshall — three pacemen. Which of them failed to register a ten-wicket haul in a Test?

Cricket Quiz Book

5) In which year did Ramadhin and Valentine bowl West Indies to their first series victory on English soil?

6) Who was the first West Indian to perform the hat trick in Tests?

7) Before Sobers two other West Indians performed the all-rounders' feat of a century and five wickets in an innings. Name them.

8) Which of the "W's" scored the most Test runs?

9) Who was the first West Indian to post a ton on his Test debut?

10) When did the West Indies poach their first series win over Australia?

NEW ZEALAND

The men from across the Tasman Sea were next to participate at the highest level.

1) What year marked the debut of New Zealand in Test cricket?

2) Who were New Zealand's first Test victims and in which year?

3) Who led the Kiwis to their first series win (overseas for good measure)?

4) In 1973 at Nottingham New Zealand piled up the highest total in a fourth innings to lose. What was the score and by how many did the Kiwis fall short?

5) Which Kiwi smashed a 30-minute half-century v. West Indies in 1968-69?

6) Brian Taylor notched three figures on Test debut as did J.E. Mills in 1929 but who scored 107 in his first appearance in 1972-73?

7) Who was the initial Kiwi to amass 100 Test strikes?

8) Which two players put together the world record tenth-wicket stand of 151 v. Pakistan in 1972-73?

9) Who produced New Zealand's first and only Test hat trick, incidentally on his debut?

10) Which "tail-end Charlie" had a fearful blow to the head (pre-helmets) which threatened his life in 1974-75, but happily recovered fully?

Cricket Quiz Book

INDIA

India became Asia's first representatives in Test cricket.

1) Who is the only batsman to chalk up a century in each of his first three Test appearances?

2) Between 1969 and 1983 how many times did Gundappa Vishwanath represent his country?

3) Which pairing possess the record opening stand of 413 in Test cricket?

4) How many Indians have known the feeling of taking nine wickets in a Test innings?

5) Which of the feared "Famous Four" spinners of the '60s and '70s never managed an eight-wicket Test innings?

6) After Kapil Dev who is the next pace bowler to remove 100 batsmen in his Test career?

7) When did India first compete in a Test match?

8) Which player shares the record for most catches in a Test innings and Test match?

9) India own the record for highest fourth innings total to win. What was the score and who suffered the reverse?

10) Who skippered the victorious Indian tourists in 1971?

PAKISTAN

The 1947 upheavals produced another Test-playing nation on the sub-continent.

1) Up to 1988 three Pakistanis have scored centuries on Test debut. Name them?

2) What is the highest score recorded by a Pakistani batsman and who made it?

3) Which pair of all-rounders put on 190 for the ninth wicket v. England in 1967?

4) In 1978-79 a stalwart produced innings figures of 9-86 against Australia. Who blitzed the Aussies?

5) Two other bowlers have removed eight batsmen in an innings. Name the pair?

6) Pakistan's first victory in England came in 1954, engineered by a match aggregate of 12-99, by whom?

7) A wicket with a first ball of a Test career is a "dream start". Whose dream came true in 1959-60?

Cricket Quiz Book

8) In 1982 a Pakistani batsman piled up 1000 runs in the calendar year. Who minced the opposition that year?

9) Younis Ahmed returned to the Test team in 1987 but when were his first two caps earned?

10) When did Pakistan record their first win over Australia? And what was unusual about it?

SRI LANKA

The newest arrivals in the top echelon have battled to establish themselves during a period of domestic turmoil.

1) i) How many Test venues are there in Sri Lanka?
   ii) How many cities host a Test?

2) Against whom and when did Sri Lanka notch their first series win?

3) Who was the victorious captain in the above?

4) In the mammoth 491-7 declared at "HQ" in 1984, who stroked a prestigious 190 before dismissal?

5) In the same match who clobbered 111 and 94 off the toiling attack?

Tests

6) The Sri Lankans are noted for batting rather than bowling — who surprised the Pakistanis with a startling 8-83 in October 1985 (in Pakistan for good measure)?

7) D.S. de Silva arrived on the Test scene at a comparatively venerable age. How far into the innings of life was he on debut?

8) Who is by far the heaviest scorer in Sri Lanka's history (as at February 1989)?

9) Among Sri Lankan Test cricketers what is by far the most popular surname?

10) Who had the honour to post the newcomer's first individual double century?

TEST CAPS

To be awarded one cap is an honour, but some players have enjoyed the experience many times. This section salutes a few of this happy band plus a couple of the less fortunate.

1) How many Tests did Sunil Gavasker play for his country?

2) Three Englishmen (February '89) have appeared in 100 Tests. Name them?

Cricket Quiz Book

3) Who are the most capped players for the following?
   i) South Africa
   ii) Pakistan
   iii) New Zealand

4) How many Tests did the following take the field in?
   i) Sir Donald Bradman
   ii) Graeme Pollock
   iii) Barry Richards

5) Who is the second Indian to pass the century?

6) Three Australian legends. How many did they rack up each?
   i) Greg Chappell
   ii) Rod Marsh
   iii) Ian Chappell

7) Geoff Howarth, one of the Kiwis' most successful skippers played how many times for his country?

8) In the celebrated Indian spin quartet of the '60s and '70s, which member tweaked the most caps?

9) Vinoo Mankad played how many Tests?

10) How many Test caps did Wale's Alan Jones receive?

Tests

ONE-CAP MEN

Some players only knew the honour once but *Wisden* will record them faithfully nevertheless.

1) Who did these men gain their one cap against?
   i) Mark Benson
   ii) Andy Lloyd

2) In which year did Sussex captain Paul Parker obtain his solitary titfer?

3) An ex-Manchester United defender took the stage, once, against the 1985 Australians. Who is the popular stalwart of two sports?

4) In the '82 series between England and India which role did G.A. Parker fulfil on one occasion?

5) Which West Indian wicketkeeper/batsman made his only appearance against the England tourists of 1985?

YOUNGEST AND OLDEST

Some Test cricketers have hardly been out of nappies while others have been almost collecting pensions — or so it seems!

1) Who was the youngest Test cricketer ever?

Cricket Quiz Book

2) Who were the youngest Test players for the following countries?
   i) India
   ii) England
   iii) West Indies

3) What age was Ian Craig when he became Australia's youngest cap?

4) J. Southerton turned out for England at Melbourne in 1876-77. How old was this gentleman?

5) Who boasts the most advanced age for anyone appearing in a Test?

TEST CAPTAINS

1) Who skippered England on these tours?
   i) Australia 1970-71
   ii) India 1972-73
   iii) Australia 1954-55

2) Captain of New Zealand in 34 consecutive tests 1955-65. Name him?

3) Who is the most successful and longest serving skipper?

4) Who has captained England more times than any other skipper?

Tests

5) The Nawab of Pataudi Junior: when did he first captain his country and when was his last captaining stint?

6) Name the skipper of the 1988 Sri Lankan tourists and their former leader who played under him?

7) Who led the West Indies in the following series?
   i) England 1973
   ii) Australia 1960-61
   iii) England 1966

8) Who came out of retirement to lead an Australian side hit by defections?

9) Which of the ensuing has the most successful ratio of wins per Test match?
   i) Mike Brearley
   ii) Clive Lloyd
   iii) Ian Chappell

10) Who was the last wicketkeeper to captain Pakistan?

11) An Australian captain resigned and left a press conference in tears. Who was he?

12) Against which nation did Geoff Boycott lead England?

Cricket Quiz Book

13) How many skippers took charge during England's 1988 series against the West Indies? And name them?

14) From 1968-1970-71 which Australian occupied the hot seat for twenty consecutive occasions?

15) How many appearances as captain did Sunil Gavaskar make?

ANSWERS

THE ASHES

1) Charles Bannerman 165 not out v. England 1876-77

2) i) Bill Woodfull
   ii) Lindsey Hassett
   iii) Bobby Simpson
   iv) Kim Hughes

3) i) 4   ii) 4   iii) 3   iv) 6

4) Australia 5-0 1920-21, England 5-1 1978-79

5) Australia Bob Simpson 311 1964, England Robert Foster 287 1903-04

6) Bob Massie 16-137 1972

7) i) once (1932-33)
   ii) once (1961)
   iii) 4 times (1972, 1976-77, 1979-80, 1981)
   iv) twice (both 1978-79)

8) Australia Sir Donald Bradman 19 , England Sir Jack Hobbs 12

9) i) 403-3 Australia 1948
   ii) 417 England 1976-77

Cricket Quiz Book

10) Bill Ponsford and Don Bradman 451 1934

11) Geoff Boycott 99 not out 1979-80

12) Terry Alderman 42 1981

13) Geoff Boycott/Alan Knott 107 and 135 respectively

14) Arthur Mailey 9-121 1920-21

15) Kepler Wessels 162 for Australia 1982-83

SOUTH AFRICA

1) 1888-89

2) 1-0 to South Africa 1965

3) Hugh Tayfield 9-113 v. England 1956-57

4) 274 — Graeme Pollock v. Australia 1969-70

5) Derrick McGlew v. Australia 1957-58

6) Alan Melville and Bruce Mitchell v. England

7) 61 (60-97)

8) Denis Lindsey

Answers

9) T.L. Goddard 2516 runs, 123 wickets

10) Dudley Nourse 208 1951

WEST INDIES

1) Lawrence Rowe v. New Zealand 1971-72 (214 and 100)

2) 9

3) John Noriega 9.95 v. India 1970-71

4) Joel Garner

5) 1950 (3-1)

6) Wes Hall v. Pakistan 1958-59

7) Denis J.T.E. Atkinson v. Australia 1954-55, O.C. "Colly" Smith v. India 1958-59

8) Everton Weekes 4,455

9) George Hedley 176 v. England 1929-30

10) 1964-65 (2-1)

NEW ZEALAND

1) 1929-30 (v. England)

2) West Indies 1955-56

3) Greg Dowling

4) 440 — 38 runs adrift

5) Brian Taylor

6) R.E. Redmond

7) Dick Motz (32 Tests)

8) Brian Hastings and Dick Collinge (110 and 68 not out)

9) Peter Petherick v. Pakistan 1976-77

10) Ewan Chatfield

INDIA

1) M. Azharrudin v. England 1984-85

2) 91

3) Vinoo Mankad (231) and Pankaj Roy (173) v. New Zealand 1955-56

4) Three. Kapil Dev v. West Indies 1983-84, J.M. Patel v. Australia 1959-60 and S.P. Gupte v. West Indies 1958-59

Answers

5) Bishen Bedi

6) Karsten Ghavri

7) 1932 v. England

8) Yarjuvindra Singh v. England 1976-77 (5 and 7)

9) 406-4 v. West Indies 1975-76

10) A.L. Wadekar

PAKISTAN

1) Khalid Ibadulla v. Australia 1964-65, Javed Miandad v. New Zealand 1976-77, Salim Malik v. Sri Lanka 1981-82

2) 337 Hanif Mohammed v. West Indies 1957-58

3) Asif Iqbal and Intikhab Alam (146 and 51)

4) Sarfraz Nowaz

5) Imran Khan (twice) and Sikander Bakht (v. India 1979-80)

6) Fazal Mahmood

7) Intikhab Alam

8) Mohsin Khan

9) 1969 v. New Zealand

10) 1956-57. It was their first encounter.

SRI LANKA

1) i)   4   ii)   2 Colombo and Kandy

2) India August/September 1985 (1-0)

3) L.R.D. Duleep Mendis

4) Sunil Wettimuny

5) Duleep Mendis

6) J.R. Ratnayake

7) 39 years 251 days

8) A. Ranatunga (1537 runs)

9) Silva, there have been 4 "De Silva's" and one "Silva"!

10) D.B.S.P. "Brendan" Kurrupu 201 not out v. New Zealand 1987

Answers

TEST CAPS

1) 125

2) Colin Cowdrey (114), Geoff Boycott (108), David Gower (100)

3) i) John Waite 50
   ii) Javed Miandad 101 (at December 1989)
   iii) Sir Richard Hadlee 86

4) i) 52   ii) 23   iii) 4

5) Dilip Vengsarkar v. New Zealand November 1988

6) i) 87   ii) 96   iii) 75

7) 47

8) Bishen Bedi 67

9) 44

10) None. His only game was against the Rest of the World (1970).

ONE-CAP MEN

1) i) India 1986   ii) West Indies 1984

2) 1981 v. Australia

Cricket Quiz Book

3) Arnie Sidebottom

4) Wicketkeeper

5) Thelston Payne

YOUNGEST AND OLDEST

1) Mushtaq Mohammed (16 years 70 days)

2) i) Sachin Tendulkar
   ii) Brian Close
   iii) J.R.D. Sealy

3) 17 years 239 days

4) 49 years 119 days — Test cricket's oldest debutant

5) Wilfred Rhodes — into his 51st year

TEST CAPTAINS

1) i) Ray Illingworth
   ii) Tony Lewis
   iii) Sir Len Hutton

2) John Reid

3) Clive Lloyd (74 Tests) 36 wins

4) Peter May 41

Answers

5) 1961-62 then finally in 1974-75

6) R.J. Madugalle and D. Mendis

7) i) Rohan Kanhoi
   ii) Sir Frank Worrell
   iii) Sir Gary Sobers

8) Bobby Simpson

9) Mike Brearley 31 Tests 18 wins, Clive Lloyd 36 wins in 74 Tests, Chappell 15 wins in 30 Tests

10) Wasim Bari

11) Kim Hughes

12) New Zealand 1977-78

13) Five. Mike Gatting, Chris Cowdrey, John Emburey, Graham Gooch and Derek Pringle when Gooch left the field injured.

14) Bill Lawry

15) 46 (9 wins)

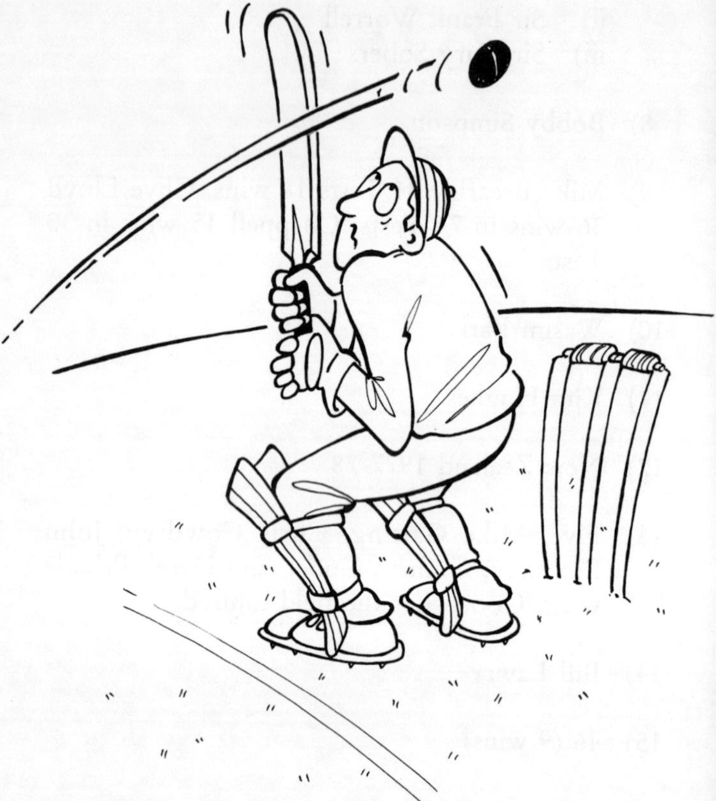

SECTION II
FEATS

1	Batting Disasters	28
2	Boundaries	28
3	Catches Win Matches	29
4	Close Ones	31
5	Ducks	31
6	Fielders	32
7	Hat Tricks	33
8	Plus "50" Averages	34
9	Run-outs	35
10	Thousand Runs Plus	35
11	The "400" Men	36
12	Wicketkeepers	37
13	Answers	40

FEATS

BATTING DISASTERS

These are the ones that no one wants to remember!

1) Who holds the undesirable feat of the lowest ever Test innings total?

2) To have one collapse appears careless but, to have two is a disaster! Which unfortunate side amassed only 34 runs from two knocks, a first-class all-time low?

3) Surrey walked into a bad day against Essex at Chelmsford in 1983. They were back in the hutch for what paltry total?

4) These are the worst Test innings for which countries?
   i)   42
   ii) 93
   iii) 53

5) Which Test side to its chagrin, has posted under 50 more times than any other?

BOUNDARIES

Smashed, stroked, snicked, nicked, hooked, cut or just played, they are all equally valuable to the side, no matter how they came.

Feats

1) Two players have achieved the ultimate six sixes in one over. Who were they and in which years did they perform it?

2) Who was signed by Glamorgan on the strength of his 13 sixes on one knock against the county in 1967?

3) Which player dispatched Malcolm Nash for 34 in one over in the 1970s?

4) Occasional bowler Kevin Sharp probably wished he hadn't bothered when this player collared him for 30 inside one over in 1987. Who was the wrecker of Sharp's figures?

5) i) Who is the only man to lash four successive sixes in a Test match?
   ii) Which bowler suffered a crick in the neck following their trajectory?

CATCHES WIN MATCHES

Cling onto them and you're a saint. Drop them and you're a sinner, no matter how difficult. Better never to have got there than to spill them. Some questions on the men with gluey not butter-fingers.

1) Who possesses the record number of catches in Tests and from whom did he take it?

Cricket Quiz Book

2) Who launched himself to a remarkable catch which literally turned the 1971 Gillette Final at Lord's?

3) Who was unlucky enough to be caught off an English foot in the 1985 Ashes series, much to skipper Border's disgust?

4) Who for some time, appeared in "Grandstands" opening titles playing "keepie-up" with a slip catch?

5) Which England wicketkeeper found himself in the unaccustomed position of the covers in a crucial 1982-83 Test, and came up with a vital catch?

6) Aside from M.C.Cowdrey, which two other Englishmen here have topped the ton in Test match victims?

7) Which Surrey player pouched seven catches in one Championship innings in 1957?

8) Who, on an average of catches per match, outstrips all other experts of the close-in sort in the modern County Championship era?

9) Who carries the record for the greatest haul of catches in an English season?

10) Only one player from the sub-continent has taken 100 Test catches. Name him.

Feats

CLOSE ONES

These matches could have caused a few coronaries but happily all the participants seem to have come out unscathed.

1) Which two Test teams produced the first tie at this level and when?

2) Who took the catch that settled a narrow England victory over the Aussies in 1982-83?

3) Which two combatants tied a one-day international in 1983-84?

4) The 1975 World Cup Final was an extremely high scoring affair and produced a tense finish. How close to victory did the last-wicket pair take Australia?

5) There was a second tied Test in 1986-87.
   i) Who were the participants?
   ii) What notch was being chased for victory?

DUCKS

"Failed to score", nought, did not trouble the scorers, early bath, a quick return to the pavilion, whichever expression you use it all amounts to nowt, the dreaded duck 007, James Bond is licensed to kill; double "O" batsman is likely to be lynched (by his team-mates).

1) Name the bowler who dismissed Sir Donald Bradman for the round figure in his last Test innings?

2) Who registered the dreaded "pair" in his debut Test at Edgbasten in 1975?

3) Another unfortunate suffered the same fate in his debut ten years on against the West Indies?

4) In 1984 who was awarded Man of the Match in the Benson and Hedges Final despite failing to trouble the scorers?

5) Who followed up a duck in his first Test knock, with a 137 in the second innings?

FIELDERS

Since the inception of one-day cricket these arts are no longer the preserve of the specialist.

1) Which positions did these men make their own?
   i) Clive Lloyd
   ii) Ian Botham
   iii) Peter Walker

Feats

2) Reckoned to be the West Indies' greatest fieldsman bar none of the '80s?

3) Fill in the missing third slip from this famous cordon: Marsh, I. Chappell, G. Chappell, _____, Mallett.

4) Fielding close to the bat one day this character took a full-blooded drive to the head, and still shouted "catch it!" while toppling backwards. Name this fearsome competitor?

5) Star Rhodesian outfielder of the 1960s. Who is he?

HAT TRICKS

Hat tricks are as rare as an uninterrupted Test series in an English summer so they should linger in the memory!

1) As at January 1989 who is the last cricketer to have done the trick in a Test?

2) Dateline 15 August 1972: Sussex batting at Eastbourne and suddenly a bowler works his magic for seven wickets in 11 deliveries (including four in five). Who was the conjurer that day?

3) How many times did F.S. Trueman perform the hat trick in his illustrious career?

Cricket Quiz Book

4) Which West Indian off-spinner achieved the feat in 1960-61? And at which ground?

5) Which bowler has had the pleasure more times than anyone else in a first-class career?

PLUS "50" AVERAGES

Sheer weight of runs is a fair indicator of ability but does not tell the whole story. There is no arguing with a fifty plus average.

1) Approximately (!) what is the first-class career average of
   i) V.J. Merchant
   ii) Lindsey Hassett.

2) Six Tests only for Pakistan yet he possesses a first-class average of 50.36 (1967-85). Who is he?

3) Which Englishman has the highest career average among his countrymen?

4) Generally to be a "great" you score 10,000 in a career. Which legend amassed only 9,921 but, at a phenomenal 69.80?

5) How many New Zealanders have averaged over 50 in a first-class career?

Feats

RUN-OUTS

Disaster for one side, delight for the other: there is no worse way to be dismissed.

1) Whose throw from the outfield removed Ian Meckiff and thus caused the first tied Test?

2) Which superlative fielder turned the 1975 World Cup Final with his deadeye accuracy?

3) In 1979 World Cup semi-final, John Wright was edging New Zealand ever closer to victory. Whose amazing work on the boundary edge sent him Wright back to the pavilion and with him the Kiwis' hopes?

4) Which players became embroiled in a major controversy during an attempted run-out in a 1971 Test?

5) What is the highest individual score which a batsman has been run out on?

THOUSAND RUNS PLUS

Some players would give their arm to notch this in a year, some tail-enders in a whole career.

1) Three players have achieved the feat of 1,000 runs *in* the month of May? Name them.

Cricket Quiz Book

2) A thousand runs *before* the end of May is a very ambitious target. Aside from the three above how many have accomplished it?

3) Who is the only man to reach the 1,000 mark before the end of May twice?

4) Which legend holds the record for runs scored in a single calendar month?

5) The highest aggregate for a calendar month outside the British Isles is 1,146. By whom and when?

THE "400" MEN

To have seen two of these a person would have to be very old, very lucky or both!

1) Who is the only player to have notched two separate scores of 400 or more?

2) When was the last occurrence in England of a 400 individual score before Graeme Hick's monumental 405 not out against Somerset in 1988?

3) What is the highest individual effort of all time? In which year was it posted?

Feats

4) How many men have had the satisfaction of registering a "400" in a first-class match?

5) The second greatest batting display of all time ended with wicket still intact; how many was it and who made it?

WICKETKEEPERS

Like soccer goalies the custodian is often considered a man apart by his fellows and a little "touched". Consequently, they deserve their own section.

1) This "stumper" appeared in just one Test in six years in the squad, then 56 more in the ensuing eight years. Name him.

2) Three illustrious Australians have snaffled 130 plus Test victims. Who are they?

3) Which counties did the following turn out for?
   i)   John Murray
   ii) Rodney Cass
   iii) George Sharp
   iv) Jimmy Binks

4) How many dismissals constituted Rod Marsh's world record in the 1982-83 series against England?

Cricket Quiz Book

5) Which pair of keepers share the record for eight dismissals in a first-class innings?

6) Who possesses the record for dismissals in the following pair of countries (all first-class matches)?
   i) West Indies   ii) India

7) Among those with 350 career victims which custodian possesses the best average per match (to 1987)?

8) Who holds India's record for Test dismissals?

9) Two Englishmen have poached over 200 Test victims. Name them?

10) Which keeper is the record-holder for removals in a *three* Test series?

11) Among "keepers" who is the top run-getter in Test cricket?

12) Which man behind the sticks has the most one-day international victims?

13) Do you remember these faithful number 2's who waited so long for a chance to shine? Which counties or countries did they serve?
   i) Andrew Brassinghen
   ii) David Nicholls
   iii) David Murray

Feats

14) Who grasped eight catches in one Benson and Hedges Cup tie in the 1982 season?

15) Which of the following has not captained a first-class side on a regular basis?
    i)   Wasin Bari   iii) Alan Knott
    ii) Ian Gould   iv) Brian Taylor

ANSWERS

BATTING DISASTERS

1) New Zealand 26 v. England 1954-55

2) Border (v. Natal East) 1959-60

3) 14

4) i) India v. England 1974
   ii) Sri Lanka v. New Zealand 1982-83
   iii) West Indies v. Pakistan 1986-87

5) South Africa 7 times

BOUNDARIES

1) Gary Sobers 1968 Notts v. Glamorgan, Ravi Shastri 1985 Baroda v. Bombay

2) Majid Khan

3) Frank Hayes

4) Matthew Maynard

5) i) Kapil Dev
   ii) Eddie Hemmings (Lord's 1990)

Answers

CATCHES WIN MATCHES

1) Greg Chappell (122) overtaking Colin Cowdrey as at February 1990

2) Jack Bond

3) Wayne Phillips

4) Graham Gooch

5) Ian Gould

6) Ian Botham and Walter Hammond

7) Micky Stewart

8) Graham Roope (602 at average 1.50 per game)

9) Walter Hammond 78 in 1928

10) Sunil Gavaskar (108)

CLOSE ONES

1) Australia and West Indies 1960-61

2) Geoff Miller (5 runs)

3) Australia and West Indies (222.8 and 222.5)

Cricket Quiz Book

4) 17 runs West Indies 291-8 Australia 274

5) i) Australia and India   ii) 348

DUCKS

1) Eric Hollies

2) Graham Gooch

3) Ken Rutherford (New Zealand)

4) John Abrahams

5) Gundappa Vishwanath

FIELDERS

1) i) Cover point   ii) Second slip
   iii) Short leg

2) Roger Harper

3) Doug Walters

4) Brian Close

5) Colin Bland

Answers

HAT TRICKS

1) Merv Hughes Australia v. West Indies December 1988

2) Pat Pocock

3) 4 times

4) Lance Gibbs — Adelaide

5) Doug Wright

PLUS "50" AVERAGES

1) i) 71 (71-22) 1929-51
   ii) 58 (58-24) 1932-53

2) Shafiq Ahmed

3) Geoff Boycott 56-83 1962-86

4) George Headley 1928-54

5) None

RUN-OUTS

1) Joe Soloman

2) Viv Richards

Cricket Quiz Book

3) Derek Randall

4) John Snow and Sunil Gavaskar

5) 499! Hanif Mohammed

THOUSAND RUNS PLUS

1) W.G. Grace 1895, Wally Hammond 1927, C. Hallows 1928

2) Five. Tom Hayward, Don Bradman, Bill Edrich, Glenn Turner and Graeme Hick

3) Don Bradman 1930 and 1938

4) Len Hutton 1,294 June 1949

5) Bill Ponsford (1927)

THE "400" MEN

1) Bill Ponsford

2) 1895 (Archie Maclaren)

3) 499 Hanif Mohammed (1959)

4) Seven. Ponsford, Hick Bradman, Mohammed, Maclaren, Aftab Baloch and B.A. Nimbulkar

Answers

5) Don Bradman 452 (1930) for New South Wales and Queensland

WICKETKEEPERS

1) Bob Taylor

2) Rod Marsh (355), Wally Grout (187), Bert Oldfield (130)

3) i) Middlesex   ii) Worcestershire
   iii) Northants   iv) Yorkshire

4) 28

5) Wally Grout Queensland v. Western Australia 1960, David East Essex v. Somerset 1985

6) i) Deryck Murray ii) Farouk Engineer

7) Ray Jennings (South Africa) 1973-87 average 3.9

8) Syed Kirmani 198 (1976-86)

9) Alan Knott 269, Godfrey Evans 219

10) Amal Silva (22) Sri Lanka v. India 1985

11) Alan Knott 4,389 runs from 95 Tests

Cricket Quiz Book

12) Jeffrey Dujon 140 plus and still going (as at February 1990)!

13) i) Gloucestershire   ii) Kent
    iii) West Indies

14) D. Taylor for Somerset v. Combined Universities

15) Alan Knott. Bari — Pakistan, Gould — Sussex, Taylor — Essex

SECTION III
THE COUNTIES

1	Derbyshire	49
2	Essex	50
3	Glamorgan	51
4	Gloucestershire	52
5	Hampshire	54
6	Kent	55
7	Lancashire	56
8	Leicestershire	57
9	Middlesex	58
10	Northamptonshire	60
11	Nottinghamshire	61
12	Somerset	62
13	Surrey	64
14	Sussex	65

Cricket Quiz Book

15	Warwickshire	66
16	Worcestershire	67
17	Yorkshire	68
18	Answers	70

THE COUNTIES

We suppose everyone identifies with at least one county. So in order not to upset anyone here are all 17 with an equal number of questions.

DERBYSHIRE

1) Who skippered the North Midlands side in their 1969 Gillette Final appearance?

2) Derbyshire have been considered a "Cinderella" county. In which year were they successful in landing the County Championship?

3) Which overseas player lifted the county from a slump in the mid-70s?

4) Which well-known post-war speed merchant was restricted to two Test caps due to a wealth of talent in the pace department?

5) How many caps did the following Derby men accrue?
    i) Alan Ward   iii) Harry Elliot
    ii) Fred Ramsey

6) Which stalwart weighed in with five hat tricks in his career?

Cricket Quiz Book

7) John Wright has been a long-term overseas player for Derbyshire. Who replaced him for 1989?

8) Which former Derbyshire player created havoc in their ranks in a 1988 one-day final?

9) Which famous overseas off-spinner graced the Derbyshire ranks in the 1970s?

10) What was W. Mycroft's feat for the county in a fixture against Hampshire in 1876?

ESSEX

1) How many years did it take Essex to win a major trophy and in which year did they break the barren spell?

2) Essex batsman A.C. Russell was the first Englishman to achieve which feat?

3) Against whom did Essex amass a record 350-3 in a Benson and Hedges Cup tie in May 1979?

4) Australian Test opening bat who joined the county in the 1970s?

5) How many County Championships have Essex secured?

The Counties

6) Essex received yeoman service from two West Indian pacemen in the 1970s. Name them and their respective tallies of caps.

7) Two thousand and eighty-two wickets in his career and now a "personality". Name him.

8) Which Essex player, whilst on tour with England was accused of cheating, allegedly using illegal substances on the ball?

9) Which recent "noted" entertainer was plucked from the obscurity of Ilford village cricket?

10) Which Essex middle-order performer became Chairman of selectors during the 1960s?

GLAMORGAN

1) Which stalwart managed to dismiss some 2,218 batsmen in a career spanning 22 years?

2) At which other sport did ex-skipper A.R. Lewis excel?

3) Which Glamorgan stumper jointly holds the record for dismissals in a NatWest trophy game?

4) What are the counties' record totals — highest

Cricket Quiz Book

and lowest — the former from 1951, the latter in 1924 (give or take 20 runs)?

5) How many years elapsed between Greg Thomas' first cap and the last previous Glamorgan appearance in an England Test side?

6) Which Test cricketer pummelled a county colleague for 30 runs in one over when on tour?

7) Who is the county's heaviest scorer in first-class cricket of all time?

8) What and when has Glamorgan's season yielded a trophy?

9) Who is the only player to produce a century on debut since the war? And what was unusual about the manner in which he attained these figures?

10) Who was the first Glamorgan player to be capped by England? And when?

GLOUCESTERSHIRE

1) Gloucestershire have been blessed with remarkable batting talent ie Grace, Jessop and Hammond. How many double centuries were scored by i) Hammond ii) Grace?

The Counties

2) Before Bill Athey's call to the colours in 1986, who was the last player to receive the summons for his country, and when?

3) How many times have the county finished second in the Championship?

4) Gloucestershire have won only two major titles — which trophies and when?

5) Which year did Courtney Walsh take his place as one of *Wisden*'s cricketers of the year?

6) The county's successes of the 1970s were based on tremendous overseas performers. Name the trio?

7) Which players hold the county records for runs scored and wickets taken?

8) Who is the most recent keeper to collect a hat trick for the county?

9) Gloucestershire players hold records for catches in a season, a match and an innings. Which player holds the last of these?

10) How many Test caps and Test centuries did Tom Graveney accumulate?

HAMPSHIRE

1) Who is Hampshire's leading run-getter of all time? And how many centuries did he accumulate?

2) What is unusual about Johnny Arnold's international record?

3) Barry Richards became the golden boy of Hampshire but which great overseas star proceeded him, scoring 1,000 runs, 18 times?

4) The Hampshire side has taken two Championships in 1961 and 1973. Name the skippers of the respective outfits?

5) Which player was a mainstay in both triumphs?

6) 1948-69 he took a massive haul of wickets but gained a paltry seven Test caps. Name him.

7) In which year did speed merchant Anderson Roberts join the county?

8) Which unwanted tag belonged to Hampshire alone, until 1988?

9) He does not hold them now, but in the 1970s one player held the highest individual scores for each major one-day competition. Who is he?

The Counties

10) Derek Shackelton posted 20 successive 100-wicket seasons, yet still a Hampshire bowler amassed more career wickets. Who was this phenomenon?

KENT

1) In 1979 and 1981 a Kent debutant scored a hundred — who were the lucky men?

2) How many times, and when was the last occasion, that Kent clinched the Championship?

3) In 1977 what was unusual about the county's Championship placing?

4) Which Kent legend is the only man to take 300 wickets in a Championship season and when?

5) The second highest run scorer in cricket history gave yeoman service to Kent. Name him.

6) How many times have Kent taken the following trophies?
   i) John Player League
   ii) Gillette/NatWest Cup
   iii) Benson and Hedges Cup

7) Which wicketkeeper holds the record for dismissals in a season?

Cricket Quiz Book

8) How many first-class hundreds did this pair reap?
   i) Colin Cowdrey
   ii) Les Ames

9) Kent were one of the first great one-day outfits, possibly because of their skill in the fielding arts. Name their uncapped player (in Tests) who nevertheless was a fixture for his outfielding?

10) Kent enjoyed great service from three great all-rounders in the 1970s. Name these three swashbucklers.

LANCASHIRE

1) When was the last occasion on which the county pocketed the Championship outright?

2) What was the top score by a Lancashire player in a first-class match?

3) What was unusual about Lancashire's victory over Leicestershire at Old Trafford in 1956?

4) Which "gloveman" has the record for dismissals for the county?

5) Before the 1989 season Lancashire lifted only one trophy under David Hughes' leadership. Which one?

The Counties

6) How many caps and Test wickets — a record for an old Trafford man — did Brian Stathan amass?

7) Before Tom Moody (1990), who was the joint-holder of the record for the fastest hundred of all time in terms of time elapsed?

8) Which brothers fill the top spots in career runs amassed for the county?

9) Cyril Washbrook obtained 37 caps — between which years?

10) Which current batsman bears the name of a legendary Australian Test cricketer?

LEICESTERSHIRE

1) Founded in 1879, none of the original members had the pleasure of seeing a trophy held aloft — how long was the wait?

2) The county took well to the Benson and Hedges Cup — which batsman scored 2,059 runs in this competition alone?

3) Before the war this bowler plundered 2,431 wickets for the county. Name him.

4) Which Leicestershire man piled up 30,225 runs between 1924-51?

Cricket Quiz Book

5) In 1959 and 1961 a Leicestershire player farmed an attack for a hundred and a double-hundred in a single match. Who was this man?

6) In 1965 Clive Inman crashed a fifty in an explosive 13 balls. How many minutes did it take?

7) Up to the '70s the county's highest Championship placing was third on two occasions — who were the respective captains?

8) Under Illingworth Leicestershire finally scaled the peak in 1975; which overseas paceman called it a day on a high note?

9) Leicestershire's record opening stand is shared by a current umpire and a noted man of Staffordshire now behind the scenes of another county. Name them.

10) Who scored exactly 100 not out on his 1986 debut?

MIDDLESEX

1) Which Middlesex bowler suffered a serious accident, but still played on for over a decade to take 2,830 wickets?

The Counties

2) Which batsman stands number three on the all-time career list with 57,011 runs?

3) How many caps did the following get?
   i)   Graeme Barlow
   ii) Wayne Daniel
   iii) Roland Butcher
   iv) Mike Selvey

4) Who became known as the terrible twins because of their coruscating strokeplay?

5) John Robertson's 331 not out represents the county's highest individual effort (1949 v. Worcestershire). What was unusual about this mammoth knock?

6) Which player retains the record for the most "tons" in a season? And how many is it?

7) Which remarkable player recorded the fourth-highest tally of wickets in a career plus 96 centuries to boot?

8) The county's top run-getter in both NatWest/Gillette and Sunday League. Who is he?

9) The 1980s have proved very successful. How many times have the following trophies been secured?
   i)   Championship
   ii) NatWest Trophy
   iii) Benson and Hedges Cup

Cricket Quiz Book

10) England's fast bowler of the '60s and '70s famed for an unusual run-up and received 15 caps. Name him.

NORTHAMPTONSHIRE

1) Who retains the record individual score for the county and how many was it?

2) Which player managed a "ton" on debut in 1985?

3) Northant's modern-day reputation is as a superb batting side. Who respectively
   i) hit 30 off an over v. Warwickshire in 1982?
   ii) smashed 12 sixes in one knock v. Gloucester in 1986?

4) Reckoned by many to be the fastest Englishman since the war, he helped Northants to their equal-best Championship position in 1957. Who was he?

5) Of whom was it said on Test debut (overheard by the man himself), "My God he is bloody grey isn't he?"?

6) How many Test caps did the devastating "Ollie" Milburn receive in his cruelly shortened career?

The Counties

7) Northants carry two of the most unwanted records in English cricket — lowest innings and lowest match aggregate. What were the offending scores?

8) Which 'keeper poached a county-best ten dismissals in a 1963 match?"

9) In total, how many trophies have made their way to the county cabinet?

10) How many Test caps did these fine overseas stars run up?
    i) Sarfraz Nawaz
    ii) Mushtaq Mohammed

NOTTINGHAMSHIRE

1) Nottinghamshire's second Championship victory was partly due to the considerable efforts of their Test opening bowlers. Who were the pairing?

2) Which player struck 209 and 146 in the same match against Middlesex in 1979?

3) Which of the one-day competitions has the county won and in what year was the triumph?

Cricket Quiz Book

4) How many England caps did the following win?
   i) Biram Bolus   iii) Bruce Dooland
   ii) Reg Simpson

5) Which spinner achieved the rare feat of removing all ten wickets when playing for an invitation XI?

6) Which Notts skipper pummelled a 48-minute century versus Sussex in 1925?

7) Versatility is the name of the game. Opening bat, middle order, wicketkeeper and sometime leg-break bowler. Who was this man of all parts during the 1970s?

8) Which two bowlers cut a swathe through the 1988 season by taking over a 100 wickets apiece?

9) Who was awarded the title International Cricketer of the Year in the winter of 1986/87?

10) Who is Notts' most capped Test player?

SOMERSET

1) Who struck the fastest hundred for the county and in which season?

The Counties

2) How many runs did Viv Richards amass in one day against Warwickshire in 1985?

3) Which player ran up 3,019 runs in first-class matches in 1961?

4) Which Somerset player four times topped 50 sixes in a season?

5) Somerset have connections with several Australians. How many caps did the following win?
   i)   Kerry O'Keese
   ii) Greg Chappell
   iii) Colin McCool

6) Who is Somerset's leading wicket-taker of all time?

7) Which bowler struck 34 times in the 1974 John Player League?

8) What is the county's highest-ever Championship placing?

9) Which "stumper" achieved eight catches in a 1982 Benson and Hedges fixture?

10) Which debutant weighed in with 117 not out against Oxford University in 1986?

Cricket Quiz Book

SURREY

1) i) How many times have Surrey been County Champions?
   ii) How many times in succession in the 1950s?

2) During 1988 which batsman contributed a century but still finished on the losing side in a one-day semi-final?

3) Four Surrey players have posted one hundred first-class centuries. Name them?

4) Which Surrey stalwart still has the fastest recorded first-class century in terms of minutes?

5) A Surrey keeper lies third on the all-time list for dismissals. Who is he?

6) Against whom did Surrey record an all-time innings low in 1983, and what was the paltry total?

7) In 1956, how many times did a Surrey bowler take all ten wickets in an innings?

8) What unique event (in England) occurred when the county played Cambridge University in 1984?

The Counties

9) Who was the skipper of their last Championship-winning side?

10) Which two international bowlers supported Laker and Lock during the 1950s reign of success?

SUSSEX

1) Who skippered the county to victory in the first two Gillette Cups?

2) Which ex-skipper rejoiced in a middle name of Troutbeck?

3) Which pair of brothers scored 34,380 and 31,716 career runs respectively?

4) Who retains the county record for a single knock?

5) Which Test batsman was forced to move on as a surplus overseas player in the 1980s?

6) Which stroke player crashed 32 of an Alvin Kallicharran over in 1982?

7) Played for England 1965-76, rated the country's fastest but often clashed with authority. Name him.

Cricket Quiz Book

8) Which Sussex bowler managed 100 wickets in a season *outside* England?

9) This man notched 100 wickets in a season 12 times post-war and was awarded five caps. Who was he?

10) How many caps did the following receive?
    i) Tony Grieg
    ii) Jim Parks (J.H.)
    iii) Rev. David Shepperd

WARWICKSHIRE

1) In 1976 a Warwicks pair hit the highest second wicket partnership in England — 465 undefeated — name the men involved?

2) In addition to Rohan Kanhai, which three West Indian colleagues joined him in the 1972 Championship side?

3) In which season did Dennis Amiss join the "100" club?

4) Who follows Amiss in the county's list of all-time run-getters?

5) Apart from R.G.D. Willis, which other England paceman did Warwicks employ in the 1970s?

The Counties

6) Which two bowlers have removed all ten in an innings since the war?

7) The highest fourth-wicket stand in English first-class cricket was established by which pair and when?

8) Which "Golden Age" giant ran up 1,000 runs in a season 24 times between 1896-1926?

9) How many centuries did the following enjoy in their careers?
    i)   R.E.S. Wyatt
    ii) W.G. Quoise
    iii) M.J.K. Smith

10) Warwicks have won the Sunday League once. When was that triumph?

WORCESTERSHIRE

1) When did the county first secure a major trophy?

2) What was the opening attack for the two 1960s Championship seasons?

3) 404-3 is the county's heaviest score in a NatWest tie. Against whom was it recorded?

Cricket Quiz Book

4) Who held the county's top score before Graeme Hick's 1988 epic?

5) Who jubilantly pulled off a double hat trick ie twice in the match against Surrey in 1949?

6) Who registered a club record 9-23 analysis v. Lancashire in 1931?

7) Who is the county's top man for effort behind the sticks?

8) Two thousand, two hundred and thirty-three wickets between 1933-55. Name him?

9) Who was the last debutant to amass a "ton" at first attempt?

10) How many one-day finals did the county contest in 1988?

YORKSHIRE

1) Yorkshire held the record for championship wins. How many and when was the last?

2) Who topped 100 wickets in a season a record 23 times?

3) Len Hutton hit 365 for England but who made 341 for the county?

The Counties

4) How many Yorkshiremen have produced 100 plus career centuries?

5) Who was Herbert Sutcliffe's partner in a record - (since beaten) opening stand of 555 in 1932?

6) Which bowler produced figures of 10.10 against Notts in 1932?

7) Which "tyke" was selected for England before the award of his county cap?

8) Yorkshire amassed a record total for a county — 887. In which season and who were the unlucky victims?

9) Among Yorkshire bowlers who managed the most hat tricks?

10) In which odd season did the county head one table and prop up another?

ANSWERS

DERBYSHIRE

1) Derek Morgan

2) 1936

3) Eddie Barlow (South Africa)

4) Les Jackson

5) i) 5   ii) 5   iii) 4

6) A.E.G. Rhodes

7) Ian Bishop (West Indies)

8) Steve Jeffries

9) S. Venkataraghavan

10) 17-103 analysis (the county best)

ESSEX

1) 103 1876-1979 (Benson and Hedges Cup)

2) Two separate hundreds in a Test

Answers

3) Combined Universities

4) Bruce Francis

5) 4 1979 1983-84 and 1986

6) Keith Boyle (21), Norbert Philip (9)

7) Trevor Bailey

8) John Lever (India 1976-77)

9) Ray East

10) Doug Insole

GLAMORGAN

1) Don Shepard

2) Rugby Union (Oxbridge Blue)

3) Terry Davies 6 v. Staffordshire 1986

4) 587-8 v. Derbyshire and 22 v. Lancashire

5) Twelve — Tony Lewis (1973)

6) Majid Khan 1967

7) Alan Jones 36,049 (1957-83)

Cricket Quiz Book

8) Championships in 1948 and 1969

9) Matthew Maynard 102 not out 1985. He attained three figures with successive sixes.

10) Maurice Turnbull 1929 (v. New Zealand)

GLOUCESTERSHIRE

1) i) 36   ii) 13

2) David Allan 1966

3) Six times

4) Gillette Cup 1973, Benson and Hedges Cup 1977

5) 1986 (118 wickets)

6) Mike Proctor, Zaheer Abbas and Sadiq Mohammed

7) C.W.C. Parker 3,278, Wally Hammond 54,896 (nearly all with Gloucester)

8) Jack Russell v. Surrey 1986

9) Tony Brown 1966 v. Northants 7

10) 79 caps 11 tons

Answers

HAMPSHIRE

1) Phil Mead (55,061) 153 centuries

2) 1 Test cap for cricket (v. New Zealand 1931) and one for soccer (v. Scotland 1933)

3) Roy Marshall

4) 1961 Colin Ingleby - Mackenzie, 1973 Richard Guilliat

5) Peter Sainsbury

6) Derek Shackelton

7) 1973

8) Never reaching a one-day final at Lord's.

9) Gordon Greenidge. John Player 163 (1979), Benson and Hedges 173 (1973), NatWest 177 (1975)

10) A.S. Kennedy (2,874)

KENT

1) Neil Taylor and Derek Aslett

2) 7 times, 1978

Cricket Quiz Book

3) It was tied for first place.

4) A.P. Tich Freeman 304 in 1928

5) Frank Woolley 58,959 (1906-38)

6) i) 3 1972-73 and 1976
   ii) 2 1967 and 1974
   iii) 3 1973, 1976 and 1978

7) Les Ames 128 in 1929

8) i) 107   ii) 102

9) Alan Ealham

10) John Shepard, Asif Iqbal and Bernard Julien

LANCASHIRE

1) 1934 (tied with Surrey in 1950)

2) Archie Maclaren 425 (1895 v. Somerset)

3) It was achieved without the loss of a wicket.

4) George Duckworth (1923-47) 1,090

5) Refuge Assurance Cup

6) 70 caps 252 wickets

Answers

7) Steve O' Shaughnessy 105 v. Leicestershire 1983

8) Ernest and John Tyldesley 38,874 and 37,897

9) 1936-56 1937 v. New Zealand to Australia 1956 (aged 42)

10) Neil Harvey Fairbrother

LEICESTERSHIRE

1) 1972 Benson and Hedges Cup, 97 years

2) Chris Bolderstone

3) W.E. Astill

4) Les Berry

5) Maurice Hallam: v. Glamorgan 210 not out and 157, v. Sussex 203 not out and 143 not out

6) 8 minutes v. Notts

7) 1952 Charles Palmer, 1967 Tony Lock

8) Graham Mackenzie

9) Barry Dudleston and John Steele 390 v. Derbyshire 1979

Cricket Quiz Book

10) Peter Bowler

MIDDLESEX

1) Fred Titmus

2) Patsy Hendren

3) i) 3   ii) 10   iii) 3   iv) 3

4) Denis Compton and Bill Edrich

5) All scored in one day (fourth highest of its kind)

6) Denis Compton 18

7) Jack (J.T.) Hearne 1888-1923 (3,061)

8) Clive Radley

9) i) Four 1980, 1982, 1985, 1990
   ii) Three 1980, 1984, 1988
   iii) Once 1986

10) John Price

NORTHAMPTONSHIRE

1) Ramon Subba Row 300 v. Surrey 1958

Answers

2) A.C. Storie v. Hants

3) i)   Alan Lamb   ii)   Roger Harper

4) Frank Tyson

5) David Steele

6) 9

7) 12 v. Gloucestershire 1907, 42 (27 and 15) 1908

8) L.A. Johnson v. Sussex

9) 2 1976 Gillette Cup, 1980 Benson and Hedges Cup

10) i)   55   ii)   57

NOTTINGHAMSHIRE

1) Harold Larwood and Bill Voce

2) Derek Randall

3) NatWest Trophy 1987

4) i)   7   ii)   27   iii)   3

5) Eddie Hemmings 1982-83 v. West Indies XI at Kingston

Cricket Quiz Book

6) A.W. Carr

7) Mike Harris

8) Franklyn Stephenson and Kevin Cooper

9) Chris Broad

10) Gary Sobers (93)

SOMERSET

1) Nigel Popplewell 1983 — 41 minutes

2) 322

3) Bill Alley

4) Arthur Wellard 1933-35-36 and 1938

5) i)   24   ii)   87   iii)   14

6) Jack White (1909-37) 2,356

7) Bob Clapp

8) Third — 5 times

9) Derek Taylor v. Combined Universities

10) Richard Bartlett

Answers

SURREY

1) i)   16   ii)   7

2) Alec Stewart

3) Jack Hobbs 197, Tom Hayward 104, Andy Sandham 107, John Edrich 103

4) Percy Fender v. Northants 1920 113 not out — 35 minutes

5) Herbert Strudwick 1,496 (1902-27)

6) 14 v. Essex

7) 3 times. Laker twice, Lock once

8) Keith Medlycott and Neil Faulkner *both* registered a hundred on debut.

9) Micky Stewart (1971)

10) Alec Bedser and Peter Loader

SUSSEX

1) Ted Dexter

2) John T. Barclay

3) John and James Langridge

79

Cricket Quiz Book

4) K.J. Duleepsinhji 333 v. Northants 1930

5) Javed Miandad

6) Paul Parker

7) John Snow

8) Maurice Tate 116 1926-27 (India/Ceylon)

9) Ian Thomson

10) i) 58   ii) 46   iii) 22

WARWICKSHIRE

1) John Jameson (240) and Rohan Kanhoi (213) v. Gloucestershire

2) Alvin Kallicharran, Deryck Murray, Lance Gibbs

3) 1986 (101 not out) v. Lancashire
4) M.J.K. Smith (39,832) 1951-75

5) David Brown

6) Eric Hollies v. Notts 1946, Jack Bannister v. Combined Services 1959

7) Alvin Kallicharran (230 n.o.) and Geoff Humpage (254) 1982 v. Lancashire

Answers

8) Billy Quaife

9) i) 85   ii) 72   iii) 69

10) 1980

WORCESTERSHIRE

1) 1964 County Championship (centenary year)

2) Jack Flavell and Les Caldwell

3) Devon 1987

4) Glenn Turner 311 v. Warwicks 1982

5) Roly Jenkins

6) Fred Root

7) Ray Booth (4,126) 1951-70

8) Reg Perks

9) David Banks v. Oxford University 1983

10) Two. NatWest Trophy and Refuge Assurance Cup

YORKSHIRE

1) 30 1968

Cricket Quiz Book

2) Wilfred Rhodes

3) George Hirst v. Leicestershire 1905

4) Geoff Boycott 151, Herbert Sutcliffe 149, Len Hutton 129

5) Percy Holmes

6) Hedley Verity

7) Brian Close

8) 1896 v. Warwickshire

9) S. Haigh (5)

10) 1983. Won Sunday League bottom of County Champs

SECTION IV
THE COUNTY SCENE

1	Around Britain	84
2	Badges	85
3	Colours and Ties	85
4	Lord's	86
5	Overseas Visitors	87
6	Transfers	87
7	Umpires	88
8	Who did They Play for?	89
9	Answers	91

THE COUNTY SCENE

First-class cricket is more than just a sport; it is a rich tapestry of tradition and lore so beloved by those who follow the game avidly.

AROUND BRITAIN

It is not just the seventeen counties of England and Wales that host the first-class game.

1) Which national side takes part yearly in the Benson and Hedges Cup?

2) Who was the last Scotsman to captain England?

3) 2 July 1969. A West Indies side complete with Clive Lloyd, Joey Carew, Basil Butcher etc, were dismissed for how many by Ireland, in a one-dayer at Sion Mills?

4) "Rice bowls and paddy fields" — a John Arlott commentary at Hampshire in the 1970s. Explain it.

5) Scotland employ a professional each season. Who was the 1988 incumbent?

The County Scene

BADGES

A chance to test how much attention you pay to the television close-ups.

1) Which county wears the Prince of Wales' feathers on their crest?

2) How many martlets on a Sussex sweater?

3) To whom do the following belong?
   i) A bear tied to a post
   ii) A running fox
   iii) A dragon

4) Two counties sport scimitars on their badges, one on a shield, one not. Which counties and which is which?

5) How many counties take a flower design as their emblem?

COLOURS AND TIES

An amazingly florid collection for a sport which is predominantly "white".

1) Name the counties whose sweaters sport the following colours.
   i) Dark green and scarlet
   ii) Oxford blue, Cambridge blue and gold
   iii) Chocolate and silver

Cricket Quiz Book

2) Two teams in action — the maroon-and-whites have defeated black-white-and-maroon. Who has beaten whom?

3) If you arrived in a yellow-red striped tie, of which club are you a member?

4) What colour ball was employed in the newly-established Refuge Assurance Cup in 1988?

5) What colour tie represents the I Zingari club?

LORD'S

A century here means just that little bit more than any other.

1) How many grounds have borne the title "Lord's"?

2) Which Middlesex player compiled 248 not out at HQ in 1981?

3) Which batsman's tally stands as the highest individual effort at HQ in a county match?

4) Who achieved his ambition of a century at Lord's in his last representative match there in 1987?

5) Who is the only overseas player to crack three Test centuries on the hallowed turf?

The County Scene

OVERSEAS VISITORS

Commonwealth visitors are commonplace but it never ceases to amaze what a far-flung family international cricket is.

1) Name the East Africans who gave yeoman service to Glamorgan and Notts respectively in the '70s.

2) Who is the current Common Market influence in the Midlands?

3) Which first-class county retained a Dutchman in 1988?

4) A county professional who gate-crashed an international all-rounders' tourney in the land of his birth. Name him and the place.

5) Kenyan-born county pro, now a New Zealand Test cap. Who is he?

TRANSFERS

Relatively uncommon in cricket but possibly a growing phenomenon.

1) A.A. Jones travelled the county scene. His first stop was Sussex but what were his other ports of call?

Cricket Quiz Book

2) Bob Willis played most of his career with Warwickshire but was involved in a long transfer wrangle moving from which county?

3) These players moved — name the losing and receiving counties in each case:
    i) Imran Khan   iii) Javed Miandad
    ii) Kapil Dev

4) Laurie Potter and Kevin Jarvis both left Kent. To whom respectively did they move?

5) Name two of Worcestershire's 1988 side who were formerly regulars at Old Trafford.

UMPIRES

The men in white are a rich crop of characters in their own right and a pretty good collection of cricketers to boot.

1) Which well-known official sat out a Test bomb-scare on the covers?

2) One current member of the Test panel did not play first-class cricket but did take part in soccer of that standard. Name him.

3) Who engages in heavy-footed ballet on "Nelson"?

The County Scene

4) Which elegant man-in-the-middle is always found under the Panama hat?

5) Name at least four current umpires who played for Yorkshire?

WHO DID THEY PLAY FOR?

A reminder of some of the famous and not-so famous and the counties they served.

1) Three South Africans who sojourned for a summer. For which counties?
   i) Vincent Van Der Bijl
   ii) Peter Swart
   iii) Anton Ferreira

2) One of the great cover points — for which county did James Clive Foat enthuse the crowds?

3) Giles and Cedric — Messrs Cheatle and Boyns — turned out for whom?

4) Two of Mrs Tunicliffe's sprogs turned out in close proximity — name them and their counties.

5) Paul Todd turned out in the minor counties between spells at which first-class counties?

Cricket Quiz Book

6) These men all represented three teams. Name the beneficiaries of their services.
   i) Mike Selvey
   ii) Younis Ahmed
   iii) Roger (R.D.V.) Knight

7) A. Jones, A.A. Jones, A.L. Jones, B.J.R. Jones and E.W. Jones. Which one avoided Glamorgan?

8) In 1980, no less than five Taylors were in action for five different counties. Name the counties.

9) West Brom fan Brian Brain left Worcestershire to join which county?

10) Little known but vital cog of a famous side. John Sullivan, middle-order for which outfit?

ANSWERS

AROUND BRITAIN

1) Scotland

2) Mike Derness

3) 25

4) John Rice the bowler, Andy Murtagh an Irish professional cricketer — circa mid-1970s

5) Clive Rice

BADGES

1) Surrey

2) 6

3) i) Warwickshire
   ii) Leicestershire
   iii) Somerset

4) Essex *with* shield, Middlesex without

5) 6. Yorkshire and Lancashire roses, Glamorgan a daffodil, Derbyshire, Hampshire and Northants variations of flower designs

91

Cricket Quiz Book

COLOURS AND TIES

1) i) Leicestershire ii) Yorkshire
   iii) Surrey

2) Kent beat Somerset

3) MCC

4) Orange

5) Red, brown, white, (fawn)

LORD'S

1) Three
   i) 1787-1810
   ii) 1809-1813
   iii) 1814 to the present

2) Wilf Slack

3) Jack Hobbs 316 not out for Surrey 1926

4) Sunil Gavaskar. Rest of World v. MCC

5) Dilip Vengsarkar

OVERSEAS VISITORS

1) John Solanky and Basharat Hassan

Answers

2) Ole Mortensen — Derbyshire

3) Hampshire (P.J. Bakker)

4) Dermot Reeve (Hong Kong)

5) Dipak Patel

TRANSFERS

1) Somerset and Middlesex

2) Surrey

3) i) Worcestershire to Sussex
   ii) Worcestershire to Northants
   iii) Sussex to Glamorgan

4) Leicestershire and Gloucestershire

5) Neil Radford and Steve O'Shaughnessy

UMPIRES

1) Dickie Bird (Lord's 1973)

2) Don Oslear

3) David Shephard

4) David Constant

Cricket Quiz Book

5) John Hampshire, Dickie Bird, Barry Leadbeater, Chris Balderstone

WHO DID THEY PLAY FOR?

1) i) Middlesex
   ii) Glamorgan
   iii) Warwickshire

2) Gloucestershire

3) Sussex and Worcestershire

4) Howard Trevor — Notts. Colin John — Derbys.

5) Nottinghamshire and Glamorgan

6) i) Surrey, Middlesex, Glamorgan
   ii) Surrey, Worcestershire, Glamorgan
   iii) Sussex, Gloucestershire, Surrey

7) B.J.R.

8) Leicestershire (Les), Derbyshire (Bob), Hampshire (Mike), Somerset (Derek), Kent (Neil)

9) Gloucestershire

10) Lancashire

SECTION V
THE TROPHIES

1	The World Cup	96
2	The Prizes	98
3	Benson and Hedges Cup	99
4	Early Championships	100
5	Gillette Cup/NatWest Trophy	101
6	Sunday League	102
7	Winners Around The World	103
8	Answers	105

THE TROPHIES

A few posers about the pots that all the efforts are aimed at.

THE WORLD CUP

1) When was the first World Cup competition held?

2) Which nations have qualified for finals and who has contested most?

3) How many players (and name them) have appeared in three finals?

4) Which nations have ended England's progress at semi-final stage?

5) Who skippered the 1983 winners?

6) Which player outscored Viv Richards at the wicket in the 1979 final?

7) Which ICC outfit contested the 1975 competition?

8) Zimbabwe are the World Cup's giant-killers. Which senior side suffered defeat at their hands?

The Trophies

9) One man turned a 1975 semi-final at Headingley single-handedly. Name him?

10) The West Indies hit a slump in 1987. Who always seemed to draw the short straw of the final over?

11) And which Pakistani tail-ender deposited him into the stand at a vital stage of a qualifying game?

12) Who scored "six and out" in the 1975 final?

13) Who returned figures of 5-15 in the 1979 showpiece?

14) Which players gave England a tremendous, if slow, opening stand in the 1979 final?

15) Who has taken part in both of England's finals?

16) Which teams hold the highest and lowest totals for the competition?

17) In 1975 a bowler came in with 1-6 from 12 overs. Name this "economist".

18) 175 not out v. Zimbabwe in 1983. Who scored it?

19) What is the lowest total to have won the trophy?

97

Cricket Quiz Book

20) Two Australians threatened to save the 1975 final at the death. Who were attempting the salvage job?

THE PRIZES

Not just in Britain but all over the world players chase trophies with their own distinctive histories and traditions.

1) Which states participate in the Sheffield Shield?

2) Who sponsored the County Championship before Britannic Assurance?

3) The NatWest Trophy replaced which domestic competitions?

4) Which competitions would the following pairs contest (first-class not one-day)?
   i)   Northern Transvaal v. Orange Free State
   ii) Otago v. Auckland
   iii) Barbados v. Leeward Islands
   iv) Railways v. United Bank

5) What is unusual about the Sharjah Challenge Cup?

6) When did Sunday League cricket first appear on our television screens?

The Trophies

7) Physically, what do the "Ashes" consist of?

8) How many teams compete each year for the World Series cup?

9) If a team completes a clean sweep of the pots available in an English season how much silverware will be accumulated?

10) What do the non-Test playing nations compete for on a regular basis?

BENSON AND HEDGES CUP

The most junior of the one-day competitions (Sunday League play-offs excepted) but no less a target.

1) Which is the only county to retain the cup?

2) Who holds the record for the highest knock (individual) over 55 overs?

3) Which county has suffered the indignity of becoming Scotland's only scalp?

4) Who is the only bowler to achieve the hat trick in a Lord's final?

5) What is the closest result in a final and when did it occur?

Cricket Quiz Book

6) Which counties have never made it to a Benson and Hedges Final?

7) Which player has smashed the competition's fastest ton?

8) Which current Somerset player set a record for catches in an innings during a stint with Combined Universities?

9) In 1987 two bowlers performed the hat trick. Name them?

10) Which side was shot out for 56 in 1982?

EARLY CHAMPIONSHIPS

The County Championship has existed as we know it since 1890, but there were competitions for many years before this date.

1) 1864-90 saw an embryo championship; which side was far and above any opposition in this period?

2) Which current minor county held a place in the earliest championships?

3) The 17-team league of today was completed by the addition of two counties in 1905 and 1921 respectively. Who are the juniors?

The Trophies

4) Four counties have never taken the title in its modern form, but which of these took the pot pre-1890?

5) 1890 saw the introduction of a points system. By what method was the champion team declared before this date?

GILLETTE CUP/NATWEST TROPHY

The granddad of one-day trophies is still packing them in after nearly 30 years.

1) Before Michael Holding's 1988 8-22 analysis, whose was the previous best effort in the competition?

2) What was unusual about the final over of the 1983 Middlesex v. Somerset semi-final?

3) Which player, ultimately on the losing side nearly put a six in the long room in the 1977 final?

4) How many overs was the original Gillette Cup tourney played over?

5) Who cracked a 77-minute century against Bedfordshire in 1968?

6) Only one side has lost successive finals. Which side and when?

Cricket Quiz Book

7) Which veteran possesses the most economical bowling return recorded?

8) Which player posted the highest score in a final?

9) Which was the first side to be defeated by a minor counties' outfit?

10) Which is the only minor side to beat first-class opposition on two occasions?

SUNDAY LEAGUE

Still spoiling the county pro's week-end after 20 years and still delighting crowds.

1) Who were the inaugural champions?

2) What is the lowest number of overs that can be bowled to achieve a result?

3) Four teams have managed three wins apiece. Who are they?

4) 8-26 remains the top analysis: who did it and when?

5) Sussex ran into a man inspired in 1970. Who took four wickets in four deliveries?

The Trophies

6) How many times have Middlesex and Surrey taken the trophy to London?

7) Who led Yorkshire to their 1983 triumph?

8) Two Essex bowlers have removed over 300 batsmen. Name the dangerous twosome.

9) Six thousand, one hundred and forty-four runs for Worcestershire. Who is he?

10) His county never pocketed the title in his playing days but he set a record for wicket-keeping. Who?

WINNERS AROUND THE WORLD

A section on the main contenders in some of the great competitions across the globe.

1) Since its inception in 1965/66 which nation has dominated the Shell Series/Red Stripe Trophy?

2) One state has taken the Ranji Trophy more times than all the other competitors together. Which was it?

3) Which three teams have monopolised the Currie Cup since 1889?

Cricket Quiz Book

4) Two competing states have yet to take the Sheffield Shield. Which two?

5) Between 1981-85 what was the common connection between the winners of the Quaid-E-Azam Trophy (ie their names)?

ANSWERS

THE WORLD CUP

1) 1975

2) West Indies (3), Australia (2), England (2), India (1)

3) Gordon Greenidge, Viv Richards, Clive Lloyd, Andy Roberts

4) Australia (1975), India (1983)

5) Kapil Dev

6) Collis King

7) East Africa

8) Australia (1983)

9) Gary Gilmour 6 wickets and second top score

10) Courtney Walsh

11) Abdul Qadir

12) Ray Fredericks — hit wicket as he heaved a six

Cricket Quiz Book

13) Joel Garner

14) Geoff Boycott and Mike Brearley

15) Graham Gooch

16) Pakistan 338-5 v. Sri Lanka 1983, Canada 45 v. England 1979

17) Bishen Bedi

18) Kapil Dev

19) 183 — India 1983

20) Dennis Lillee and Jeff Thomson

THE PRIZES

1) South Australia, West Australia, Queensland, Victoria, New South Wales and Tasmania

2) Schweppes

3) Gillette Cup

4) i)   Currie Cup
   ii) Plunket Shield
   iii) Red Stripe Trophy
   iv) Quaid-E-Azam Trophy

5) It is held in Dubai.

Answers

6) 1969

7) The remains of bails used in an early Test match.

8) Three

9) Five since the addition of the Refuge Assurance Cup.

10) International Cricket Conference Trophy

BENSON AND HEDGES CUP

1) Somerset 1981/82

2) Graham Gooch 198 (n.o.) v. Sussex 1982

3) Lancashire 1986 (3 runs)

4) Ken Higgs Leicestershire v. Surrey 1974

5) Yorkshire v. Northants 1987. Scores tied Yorks winning on wickets intact: 244-6 — 244-7

6) Glamorgan and Sussex

7) Malcolm Nash Glamorgan v. Hants (62 runs) 1976

8) Vic Marks 5 (v. Kent 1976)

Cricket Quiz Book

9) Neil Mallender Sussex v. Combined Universities, Winston Benjamin Leicestershire v. Notts

10) Leicestershire v. Minor Counties

EARLY CHAMPIONSHIPS

1) Nottinghamshire 15 titles outright or shared

2) Cambridgeshire 1864-69 and 1871

3) Northamptonshire (1905), Glamorgan (1971)

4) Gloucestershire

5) The team with the fewest defeats.

GILLETTE CUP/NATWEST TROPHY

1) Derek Underwood Kent v. Scotland 8.31 (1987)

2) Ian Botham blocked each ball to achieve a Somerset win on less wickets lost — scores tied.

3) Mike Llewellyn Glamorgan v. Middlesex

4) 65

Answers

5) Roy Marshall — Hampshire

6) Kent. 1983 — lost to Somerset by 24 runs, 1984 — lost to Middlesex by 4 wickets

7) Jack Simmons (12-9-3-1) v. Suffolk 1985

8) Geoffrey Boycott 146 v. Surrey 1965

9) Yorkshire v. Durham 1975

10) Durham. The above plus Derbyshire in 1985.

SUNDAY LEAGUE

1) Lancashire

2) 20. 10 overs per side

3) Hampshire, Essex, Worcestershire and Lancashire

4) Keith Boyce 1971 v. Lancashire

5) Alan Ward for Derbyshire

6) Never

7) Ray Illingworth

8) Stuart Turner and John Lever

9) Glenn Turner

10) Bob Taylor Derbyshire

WINNERS AROUND THE WORLD

1) Barbados

2) Bombay (30 times)

3) Western Province, Natal and Transvaal

4) Queensland and Tasmania

5) Banks. United Bank 1981-83-85. National Bank 1982 and 1986.

SECTION VI
GREAT PLAYERS

1	Sir Donald Bradman	115
2	Denis Compton	115
3	Ian Botham	116
4	Geoff Boycott	117
5	Richie Benaud	117
6	Sydney (S.F.) Barnes	118
7	Bhagwant Chandrasekher	118
8	Sir Learie Constantine	119
9	Greg Chappell	119
10	Kapil Dev	120
11	Sunil Gavaskar	121
12	W.G. Grace	121
13	David Gower	122
14	Lance Gibbs	123

15	Clarrie Grimmett	123
16	"Patsy" Hendren	124
17	Sir Jack Hobbs	124
18	Sir Len Hutton	125
19	Michael Holding	125
20	Sir Richard Hadlee	126
21	Walter Hammond	127
22	Imran Khan	127
23	Jim Laker	128
24	Ray Lindwall	129
25	Dennis Lillee	129
26	Clive Lloyd	130
27	"Vinoo" Mankad	130
28	Mushtaq Mohammed	131
29	Keith Miller	131
30	Javed Miandad	132
31	Mike Proctor	132

32	Barry Richards	133
33	Viv Richards	133
34	Wilfred Rhodes	134
35	Sir Garfield Sobers	135
36	Zaheer Abbas	135
37	Frank Woolley	136
38	Gundappa Vishwanath	136
39	Glenn Turner	137
40	Bill Pansford	137
41	Sir Frank Worrell	138
42	Everton Weekes	138
43	Doug Walters	139
44	Rodney Marsh	139
45	John Snow	140
46	Derek Underwood	141
47	F.E. Spofforth	141
48	Fred Trueman	142

49	Graeme Pollock	142
50	Gordon Greenidge	143
51	Answers	144

GREAT PLAYERS

No introductions are needed. Hopefully we will not offend too many people with those we have left out.

SIR DONALD BRADMAN

1) Apart from the obvious, what was the significance of the Don's failure to score in his last Test knock?

2) How many treble-hundreds did the "Don" knock up in his career?

3) He reached his hundredth hundred nearly twice as quickly as anyone else. How many innings did it take?

4) In which series did the "Don" cane the attack for a mammoth 974 runs?

5) Which two sides benefited from his colossal talent in the Sheffield Shield?

DENIS COMPTON

1) What is Denis Compton's
   i) highest Test score?
   ii) highest first-class knock?

2) How many tons did the Middlesex star compile?

3) When did Compton and Edrich amass their 424 English record stand?

4) Of the then Test-playing nations, which did D.C.S. fail to notch a Test century against?

5) In which year did Compton crack 1,000 Test runs in a year?

IAN BOTHAM

1) In how many Tests did Botham achieve the coveted "double"?

2) Ian Botham holds the record for six hits in an English season (1985). How many times did he send the spectators scurrying?

3) What is Botham's highest Test score and who suffered?

4) How many times, and when has "Both" taken 100 wickets in a season?

5) For how many series was Botham captain?

Great Players

GEOFF BOYCOTT

1) What is Geoff Boycott's highest Test score?

2) How many Test hundreds did he compile?

3) On how many occasions did he captain England?

4) How many runs has this master batsman amassed (approximately) in a i) Test career ii) first-class career?

5) Geoffrey holds only one of Yorkshire's partnership records. Which one?

RICHIE BENAUD

1) Richie Benaud removed five batsmen in an innings 16 times in Tests, but how many ten-wicket matches did he have?

2) How many Tests did it take him to reach the "double"?

3) What was Benaud's final tally of Test wickets?

4) What all-rounder's achievement was Benaud first to manage in Test cricket?

Cricket Quiz Book

5) When and against whom did Richie take part in his final Test?

SYDNEY (S.F.) BARNES

1) What was remarkable about S.F.'s 49 wickets in a series in 1913-14?

2) In the same series Barnes posted the then record analysis for Test cricket. One hundred and fifty-nine runs conceded for how many wickets?

3) Sydney Barnes played only 27 Tests — over what period?

4) Sydney's Test wickets not only came quickly but at a miserly average. Approximately what was it?

5) In a spell during the Melbourne Test of 1911-12 how many Aussies did Barnes remove at the cost of one run?

BHAGWANT CHANDRASEKHER

1) What childhood illness caused this great bowler's withered left arm?

2) How many Tests did he require to amass his 242 Test wickets?

Great Players

3) Chandra is the only Indian to dismiss 35 batsmen in a series. Who suffered and when?

4) Chandra lies second to Kapil Dev in the number of five-wicket innings registered in Tests. How many times did he pull off the feat?

5) Which England Test opener was totally surprised by a bouncer from the spinner in an Edgbaston Test?

SIR LEARIE CONSTANTINE

1) When did Sir Learie receive his Knighthood?

2) From which Caribbean Island did he hail?

3) Sir Learie Constantine performed one of the rarest of all-rounders' feats against Northants in 1928. Recorded only ten times, what was it?

4) What was the great man's highest Test score?

5) How many i) Tests ii) wickets did Sir Learie run up in his career?

GREG CHAPPELL

1) Which player did Greg, as captain, order to

bowl an underarm delivery in a one-day international?

2) In 1973-74 Chappell caned the New Zealanders for a hundred and a double-hundred in a match. The latter is his highest Test effort — what score is it?

3) He cracked a ton on Test debut; in which season and against whom?

4) Which county benefited from his services before his Test career?

5) What was unique about Greg's hundred in the 1972 Test against England at the Oval?

KAPIL DEV

1) Kapil's bowling effort at Ahmadabad in 1983-84 represents the second best innings return by an Indian bowler. How many wickets and against whom?

2) For which two English counties has Kapil played?

3) How many Tests did he take to reach the "double" 23, 25 or 27?

4) Kapil is the only Indian to crash 300 runs and

Great Players

take 20 wickets in a Test series. Which side took it on the chin and when?

5) Kapil's top score of 193 was achieved for his Indian side which has never won the Ranji Trophy but has reached the final under his guidance. Name the side?

SUNIL GAVASKAR

1) How many hundreds did "Sunny" make for India?

2) Only once did he carry his bat in a Test innings. Who was it against, how many did he score?

3) On how many occasions did he score two hundreds in the same Test match?

4) Approximately, what was his average for the 1970-71 series against the West Indies?

5) Which county landed his services in England?

W.G. GRACE

1) W.G. once retired on 93 not out. What was his reason?

2) How many times did the doctor captain his country?

3) How many players have scored more runs in a first-class career than W.G.?

4) Not only was the doctor the first man to hit a triple hundred, he did it twice in the same season for good measure. Which year?

5) At what age did W.G. reach his hundredth hundred?

DAVID GOWER

1) David Gower hit the record one-day international score for an Englishman. How many and against whom?

2) How many times did "Lulu" pass 150 in the 1985 series with Australia?

3) When did he first captain England?

4) How many Tests did he require to reach his 7,000 Test runs?

5) After which tour was Gower awarded the title International Cricketer of the Year?

Great Players

LANCE GIBBS

1) When Warwickshire tied on points (but lost on wins) for the 1971 County Championship, what was Gibbs' massive wicket haul?

2) In what year did Lance overtake Fred Trueman's world record for Test wickets?

3) How many Tests did he play and what was the span of his career?

4) Which spin king did Gibbs replace in the Guyanese Shell Shield side?

5) Who is Gibbs' famous Test-playing cousin?

CLARRIE GRIMMETT

1) With whom did Grimmett for so long share the spinning duties for Australia?

2) Grimmett destroyed one nation with 14 and 13 wickets in two Tests. Who suffered?

3) In a scintillating display of the leg spinner's art, Grimmett removed a county side with an innings analysis of 10-37. Which county and on what tour?

4) Grimmett was originally a native of which country?

Cricket Quiz Book

5) Two hundred and sixteen Test wickets from amazingly few Tests. How few?

"PATSY" HENDREN

1) How many centuries did this joker amass and when did he post the hundredth?

2) He made only one triple century but a massive number of doubles. How many?

3) In 1923, 1927 and 1928 Hendren scored the same number of centuries — his best. How many did he produce?

4) In which overseas country does "Patsy" still hold the record for runs in a season?

5) Two Hendren "figures" to finish:
   i) How many Test caps?
   ii) In how many seasons did he top 3000 runs?

SIR JACK HOBBS

1) Sir Jack's only triple hundred came against Middlesex. In which year?

2) How many of his amazing 197 tons came in Tests?

Great Players

3) With whom did the "Master" share a 428 opening stand against Oxford University in 1926?

4) 1925 saw him record how many tons? And whose record for career centuries did he pass?

5) What was the length of his Test career?

SIR LEN HUTTON

1) How many triple hundreds in Sir Leonard's career?

2) Seventy-nine Tests for England but what was his total as captain?

3) What injury did he have to overcome to continue his career after the war?

4) What was the span of the Yorkshire opener's i) Test career? ii) county career?

5) Approximately what were his career totals?

MICHAEL HOLDING

1) Holding's 14-149 represents the best effort by a West Indian in England. In which year and on which flat track?

125

Cricket Quiz Book

2) In what other sport was "Whispering Death" a national champion?

3) Holding has played regularly in four countries — England, Australia, New Zealand, and of course the West Indies. Who has employed him in each case?

4) With his formidable hitting he has approached all-rounder class. What is his highest Test knock?

5) How many World Cup finals has this great bowler appeared in?

SIR RICHARD HADLEE

1) Up to December 1988 how many times — a record — has "Paddles" rocked up a ten-wicket match in Tests?

2) In which season did he achieve the coveted and now rare "double" in county cricket?

3) Which is Sir Richard's top haul of wickets in a single Test?

4) In addition to his bowling prowess he is a feared batsman. What is his highest Test score?

Great Players

5) How many Test matches did Sir Richard play alongside his brother Dale?

WALTER HAMMOND

1) "Wally" holds the record for most runs in a series by an Englishman — 905 — scored in which year of which attack?

2) What was his best score in both Tests and all forms of cricket?

3) Elsewhere in this book are Hammond's catching efforts; he also poached a fair number of Test wickets — the total?

4) No Englishman has hit more runs in a Test match day. How many did he smash to establish the record?

5) How many triple centuries did the Gloucestershire man compile?

IMRAN KHAN

1) What was Richie Benaud's term for the vicious inswinger, Imran made his trademark in Australia?

Cricket Quiz Book

2) Along with Ian Botham Imran has performed a massive Test feat for an all-rounder. Against India in 1982-83 what was it?

3) How many times has Imran produced a ten-wicket match for his country?

4) What are Imran's best performances in Tests
   i) for bowling match figures?
   ii) for batting?

5) Where did Imran take 6-14, a Pakistan best, in a one-day international in 1984-85?

JIM LAKER

1) When Laker took his 19-wicket haul in the 1956 Old Trafford Test, who took the only other wicket?

2) In 1950 Jim Laker delivered 14 overs for England v. The Rest at Bradford in a remarkable spell conceding two runs for what number of wickets?

3) How many Tests did he play?

4) In the historic 1956 series v. Australia what was his final tally of wickets?

5) What was the great spinner's final total of Test victims?

Great Players

RAY LINDWALL

1) How many tours to England did the formidable Lindwall make?

2) At what age did he finally take his leave of Test cricket?

3) What was the final tally of Test wickets?

4) One of seven Aussies to establish the "double" in Tests — how many Tests did he take and what was his tally of runs (approximately)?

5) How many Tests 10-wicket hauls did Lindwall have?

DENNIS LILLEE

1) For how many seasons was Lillee rendered incapable of adding to his haul of Test victims by a serious back injury?

2) Lillee's 300 Test victims came in the fewest number of matches. How many?

3) How many wickets did this controversial character take in the 1981 Ashes series?

4) With which world-class player did Lillee have

Cricket Quiz Book

a dust-up in front of millions of viewers, aiming a kick in his direction?

5) What is his top haul from a single Test innings?

CLIVE LLOYD

1) When did "Hubert" make his Test debut?

2) What is the Guyanese star's top Test score?

3) When was Lloyd named as one of *Wisden*'s Cricketers of the Year?

4) How many Test wickets did Clive's gentle medium-pace notch?

5) In 1976 for West Indies, Lloyd pummelled 201 not out in a record-equalling number of minutes. How long?

"VINOO" MANKAD

1) "Vinoo" was a nickname. What was the player's real name?

2) How many Tests did it take "Vinoo" to reach the coveted "double"?

3) In which season did he perform the double?

Great Players

4) How many Tests did he play for his country?

5) How many times did "Vinoo" demolish a Test team with eight wickets in one innings?

MUSHTAQ MOHAMMED

1) What is the ex-Pakistani captain's top Test score?

2) What was unusual about his performance in the above match?

3) How many centuries were accrued in his first-class career?

4) How many Tests did "Mushy" appear in and how many wickets did he acquire?

5) How many triple-hundreds did this wearer of outlandish hats compile?

KEITH MILLER

1) How many Test centuries did Miller, who preferred it to bowling, produce?

2) Miller's Test double arrived in what time?

3) Approximately what was Miller's overall Test batting average?

Cricket Quiz Book

4) What was his total of ten-wicket matches in Tests?

5) All Miller's Test hundreds came against two nations. Which two?

JAVED MIANDAD

1) How many times, and against whom has Javed passed 250 in a Test knock?

2) What did Javed notch on his Test debut?

3) In what year did he first captain the Pakistani national side?

4) Javed jointly held the record for any partnership in Test cricket; what is the total and who did he share it with?

5) When was he one of the five *Wisden* Cricketers of the Year?

MIKE PROCTOR

1) Which rare feat has the mighty Proctor managed, shared with C.B. Fry and Don Bradman?

2) What was odd about Proctor's hat trick against Essex in 1972?

Great Players

3) How many Test appearances was he limited to?

4) In those appearances how many wickets did he gather?

5) Roughly how many wickets did Proctor amass in his 15-year career at Gloucestershire?

BARRY RICHARDS

1) How many double-hundreds did Richards score for Hampshire?

2) His top score is 356 for South Australia against Western Australia in 1970-71. How many did he compile in one day?

3) How many first-class tons did the sparkling South African amass?

4) His 28,538 career runs come at an excellent average. Roughly what?

5) What was this great batsman's career span?

VIV RICHARDS

1) In 1985 who was caned for 325 in a day by the great man?

Cricket Quiz Book

2) In which series did Viv pile up 829 runs in only 4 matches?

3) When did he first take charge of a West Indies side for a whole series?

4) Which Lancashire league side signed him on after the bust-up with Somerset?

5) As at January 1989, how many hundreds has I.V.A. scored?

WILFRED RHODES

1) How many — a record — County Championship matches did Rhodes appear in?

2) Which batting position did Rhodes begin his career in, and where did he end it?

3) How many times did Rhodes perform the "double" in county cricket?

4) The heaviest wicket-taker of all time — how many did he take?

5) Against whom and in which year did he return a Test best 15-124?

Great Players

SIR GARFIELD SOBERS

1) Who were on the receiving end of the 365 record Test score?

2) How many times did he make the coveted double of ton and five wickets in an innings, in a Test?

3) In 93 Tests Sobers ran up
   i) how many runs?
   ii) how many wickets?

4) How many Test hundreds did this phenomenon score?

5) How many ten-wicket matches did this great all-round bowler get?

ZAHEER ABBAS

1) Zaheer has cracked two tons in a match a record number of times. What is his record?

2) In addition this amazing run-getter compiled a ton and double-ton on how many occasions?

3) What is Zed's top Test score and who had to watch it?

4) How many centuries did Zed produce in his first-class career?

5) The prolific star hit 2,306 runs in 1981 at what average (approximately)?

FRANK WOOLLEY

1) What method of delivery did he employ for his 2,068 wickets?

2) Where does Woolley stand on the all-time list of run-getters?

3) How many times did the Kent stalwart crack 3,000 runs in a season?

4) Between 1909-26 Woolley piled up how many consecutive Test appearances?

5) Never the most consistent Test player Woolley's top of 154 was scored against which team?

GUNDAPPA VISHWANATH

1) Which record does "Vishy" share with Dirk Wellhem of Australia?

2) How many Test appearances did he make for India?

Great Players

3) What was unusual about the 415 added by Vishwanath in the 1981-82 Madras Test v. England?

4) How many career hundreds did the little man make?

5) What was his highest Test innings?

GLENN TURNER

1) How many times did the opener carry his bat through a New Zealand innings?

2) In which season did Turner achieve his 1,000 runs before the end of May?

3) What was unique about his 141 not out against Glamorgan in 1977?

4) Against whom did he plunder a then record 171 not out in a one-day international?

5) What is his Test best?

BILL PANSFORD

1) Despite two 400 plus first-class efforts his highest Test score is below 300. What is it?

2) Pansford's career spanned how many years?

3) Who was his regular opening partner for Victoria?

4) How many career hundreds did Pansford amass?

5) What was his share of Victoria's record 1,107 against New South Wales in 1926?

SIR FRANK WORRELL

1) In what year did Sir Frank skipper the West Indies to a 3-1 victory in England?

2) How many Test wickets did he amass?

3) Roughly what was the great man's first-class average?

4) How many Test hundreds did he produce?

5) With Clyde Wolcott, what was their West Indies domestic record partnership posted in 1945-46?

EVERTON WEEKES

1) In which season did "E de C" manage five tons in successive matches?

Great Players

2) What is his highest Test score and whose attack took the punishment?

3) Uniquely, what record does he hold starting in 1947-48, completed in 1948-49?

4) How many Test tons did he hit?

5) What was Weekes' average for the 1952-53 series v. India?

DOUG WALTERS

1) Walters was the first man to do what in Tests?

2) How many did he get on Test debut?

3) Who suffered his Test best of 250 and when?

4) How many Test wickets did his "golden arm" produce?

5) How many Test hundreds did he manage in England?

RODNEY MARSH

1) Which state has Rod skippered in the Sheffield Shield?

Cricket Quiz Book

2) How many Test tons has the "stumper" supplied?

3) What is his record number of Test victims?

4) How many of the above total are stumpings?

5) Which one-day milestone was Marsh the first to reach?

JOHN SNOW

1) What were
   i) Snow's number of Tests?
   ii) the span of these appearances?

2) He had only one ten-wicket Test. Where and when?

3) What was his number of victims in the 1970-71 series in Australia?

4) With whom did he compile a 128 last wicket stand in 1966?

5) Until 1975 his best figures had been against a touring side — 7-29. Which tourists and when?

Great Players

DEREK UNDERWOOD

1) Against whom did "Deadly" carve out 8.51 on a dutifully wet track?

2) How many times did he register a ten-wicket bag in Tests?

3) Despite three years in WSC how many wickets short of 300 in Tests did the Kent man fall?

4) In which country did he return 15-43 in a select match?

5) How many times did this demon spinner take 100 wickets in a season?

F.E. SPOFFORTH

1) He played comparatively few Tests. How many?

2) In 1882 at the Oval he demolished the English batting. What were his match figures?

3) What remarkable feat did the "demon" achieve in a non-first-class match in 1881-82?

4) In the 1878-79 Melbourne Test he became the first player to do what?

Cricket Quiz Book

5) In his small number of Tests how many ten-wicket hauls did he get?

FRED TRUEMAN

1) How many first-class centuries did this great bowler make?

2) How many times did F.J. perform the hat trick in his career?

3) On which ground and what year, did he reach 300 Test wickets?

4) What was his career total of wickets?

5) For how long did his record of Test victims endure?

GRAEME POLLOCK

1) How many Tests did Pollock get in before the South African's exile?

2) What is his remarkable Test average?

3) How old was Pollock when he hit his first double hundred?

4) With whom did he pile on 341 for a third wicket — a South African record in Tests?

Great Players

5) What is his record Test score for a South African?

GORDON GREENIDGE

1) How many double centuries did Greenidge compile against England in 1984?

2) Which other Test side could Gordon have played for?

3) What did Greenidge score in his first two Test innings?

4) What is Greenidge's highest knock in the following?
   i) John Player League
   ii) Benson and Hedges Cup

5) For which Red Stripe Trophy side does Gordon turn out?

ANSWERS

SIR DONALD BRADMAN

1) It prevented him ending with a Test average of 100.

2) Six

3) 295 (next best Denis Compton 552)

4) 1930 versus England

5) New South Wales and South Australia

DENIS COMPTON

1) i) 278 v. Pakistan 1954
   ii) 300 for MCC v. N.E. Transvaal 1948/49

2) 123

3) 1948 Middlesex v. Somerset

4) India

5) 1948

Answers

IAN BOTHAM

1) 21

2) 80

3) 208 v. India 1982

4) 1978. Once

5) 2 v. West Indies 1980 and 1980/81

GEOFF BOYCOTT

1) 246 not out v. India 1967

2) 22

3) Four times: once v. Pakistan, three v. New Zealand (1977-78)

4) i) 8,114 runs ii) 48,426 runs

5) The tenth, 149 with Graham Stevenson v. Warwickshire 1982

RICHIE BENAUD

1) One 11-105 v. India 1956/57

2) 32

3) 248 and 63

4) 2,000 runs and 200 wickets

5) 1963 v. South Africa

SYDNEY (S.F.) BARNES

1) There were only four Tests.

2) 17

3) 1901-1914

4) 16.43

5) Four. Bondsely, Kellaway, Hill and Armstrong

BHAGWANT CHANDRASEKHER

1) Polio

2) 58

3) England 1972-73

4) 16

Answers

5) Dennis Amiss

SIR LEARIE CONSTANTINE

1) 1962

2) Trinidad

3) A century and a hat trick in the same match.

4) 90 v. England 1934/35

5) i) 18   ii) 58

GREG CHAPPELL

1) Trevor Chappell

2) 247 not out

3) 1970-71 v. England

4) Somerset

5) The only occasion brothers have hit centuries in the same Test innings.

KAPIL DEV

1) 9-83 v. West Indies

2) Northants and Worcestershire

3) 25

4) England 1981-82 (318 runs, 22 wickets)

5) Haryana

SUNIL GAVASKAR

1) 34

2) 127 v. Pakistan 1982-83

3) Three times: v. West Indies 1970-71, v. Pakistan 1978-79, v. West Indies 1978-79

4) 154.80 (774 runs)

5) Somerset

W.G. GRACE

1) This was the only first-class score below a hundred he had not registered.

2) 13

3) Four

4) 1876

Answers

5) 1895 aged 47

DAVID GOWER

1) 158 v. New Zealand 1982-83

2) Three times 157, 166, 215

3) V. Pakistan 1983-84

4) 100

5) 1982-83 in Australia

LANCE GIBBS

1) 131

2) 1976

3) 79 (1958-76)

4) Sunny Ramadhin

5) Clive Lloyd

CLARRIE GRIMMETT

1) Bill O'Reilly

Cricket Quiz Book

2) South Africa 14-199 1931-32 and 13-173 1935-36

3) Yorkshire 1930

4) New Zealand

5) 37

"PATSY" HENDREN

1) 170 (1928-29)

2) 22

3) 13

4) West Indies 1929-30 1765 runs (average 135.26)

5) i) 51   ii) 3

SIR JACK HOBBS

1) 1926 (316 not out)

2) 15

3) Andy Sandham

4) 16 (W.G. Grace)

Answers

5) 1909-30

SIR LEN HUTTON

1) One. The famous 364

2) 23

3) Left-arm shorter

4) i) 1937-55   ii) 1934-60

5) 6,971 and 40,140

MICHAEL HOLDING

1) 1976 at the Oval

2) Athletics

3) Jamaica, Lancashire/Derbyshire, Tasmania and Canterbury

4) 73 v. England

5) Two 1979 and 1983

SIR RICHARD HADLEE

1) Nine

2) 1984

3) 15-123 v. Australia 1985-86

4) 151 not out v. Sri Lanka 1986-87

5) Ten

WALTER HAMMOND

1) 1928-29 v. Australia

2) 336 not out v. New Zealand 1932-33

3) 83

4) 295 v. New Zealand as above

5) Four

IMRAN KHAN

1) "Inshoot"

2) A century and ten wickets in a match 112, 6-98 and 5-82

3) Six times

4) i) 14-116 v. Sri Lanka 1981-82

ii)   135 not out v. India 1986-87

5) Sharjah

JIM LAKER

1) Tony Lock
2) 8
3) 46
4) 46
5) 193

RAY LINDWALL

1) Three: 1948, 1953 and 1956
2) 38
3) 228
4) 38 and 1,502
5) None

DENNIS LILLEE

1) Two. 1972 and 1973

Cricket Quiz Book

2) 56

3) 39

4) Javed Miandad

5) 7-83 v. England 1981

CLIVE LLOYD

1) 1966-67 v. India

2) 242 not out v. India 1974-75

3) 1970

4) 10

5) 120 minutes

"VINOO" MANKAD

1) Mulvantri

2) 23

3) 1946

4) 44

5) Twice: 8-52 v. Pakistan 1952-53 and 8-55 v. England 1951-52

Answers

MUSHTAQ MOHAMMED

1) 201 v. New Zealand 1972-73

2) Only the second time a player has scored a double ton and taken five wickets in one innings (5-49).

3) 72

4) 57 and 79

5) One. 300 not out for Karachi Blues v. Karachi University 1967-68

KEITH MILLER

1) Seven

2) 33

3) 36.97

4) One. 10-152 v. England 1956

5) Three v. England, four v. West Indies

JAVED MIANDAD

1) 280 not out v. India 1982-83, 260 v. England 1987 and 271 v. New Zealand 1988-89

2) 163 1976-77

3) 1981-82

4) 451 with Mudassar Nazar for the third wicket v. India 1982-83

5) 1981

MIKE PROCTOR

1) 6 successive centuries in successive matches in 1970-71.

2) All leg before wicket

3) 7

4) 41

5) 814

BARRY RICHARDS

1) Three

2) 325

3) 80

4) 54.74

Answers

5) 1964-82

VIV RICHARDS

1) Warwickshire
2) V. England 1976
3) 1984-85 v. New Zealand
4) Rishton
5) 100

WILFRED RHODES

1) 763
2) Number 11 to opener
3) 16
4) 4,187
5) Australia 1903-0

SIR GARFIELD SOBERS

1) Pakistan 1957-58

Cricket Quiz Book

2) Twice: v. India 1961 and v. England 1966

3) i)   8,032   ii)   235

4) 26

5) 0 (none)

ZAHEER ABBAS

1) Eight (8)

2) Four: v. Surrey and Kent 1976, v. Sussex 1977 and Somerset 1981

3) 274 v. England 1971

4) 107

5) 88.69

FRANK WOOLLEY

1) Left-arm slow

2) Second to Jack Hobbs

3) Once

4) 52

5) V. South Africa

Answers

GUNDAPPA VISHWANATH

1) A century on both first-class and Test debut.

2) 91

3) Three players were involved due to a retirement.

4) 44

5) 222 v. England in 1981

GLENN TURNER

1) Twice v. England 1969 (43 out of 131) and v. West Indies 1971/72 (223 of 368)

2) 1973

3) 141 out of 169 no-one else in double figures — 83-4% of the total highest slice by any one man in a first-class innings.

4) East Africa 1975

5) 259 v. West Indies 1971-72

BILL PANSFORD

1) 266 v. England 1934

2) 1920-1934

3) Bill Woodfull

4) 47

5) 352

SIR FRANK WORRELL

1) 1963

2) 69

3) 54.24

4) 9

5) 574 undefeated Barbados v. Trinidad

EVERTON WEEKES

1) 1955-56

2) 207 v. India 1952-53

3) Five successive Test centuries

4) 15

5) 102.28

Answers

DOUG WALTERS

1) A hundred and a double-hundred in the same Test 1968-69 v. West Indies (242 and 103)

2) 155

3) New Zealand 1976-77

4) 49

5) 0

RODNEY MARSH

1) Western Australia

2) Three

3) 355

4) 12

5) 1000 runs and 100 dismissals (1220 and 123)

JOHN SNOW

1) i) 49   ii) 1965-76

2) 1967/68 v. West Indies

3) 31

4) Ken Higgs v. West Indies (Snow 59 not out)

5) 1966 West Indies

DEREK UNDERWOOD

1) V. Pakistan 1974

2) Six occasions

3) Three

4) Sri Lanka 1967-68 for International XI against Presidents XI

5) Ten times

F.E. SPOFFORTH

1) 18

2) 14-90

3) All 20 wickets for 48 runs

4) Take a hat trick.

5) Four

Answers

FRED TRUEMAN

1) Three

2) Four

3) 1964 v. South Africa at the Oval

4) 2,304

5) 11 years, 1965-76

GRAEME POLLOCK

1) 23

2) 60.97

3) 19 years old

4) Eddie Barlow v. Australia 1963-64

5) 274 v. Australia 1969-70

GORDON GREENIDGE

1) Two

2) England

3) 93 and 107

Cricket Quiz Book

4) i) 163   ii) 173

5) Barbados

SECTION VII
A MIXED BAG

1	Aristocracy	167
2	Bodyline	168
3	Commentators	168
4	Double-barrellers	170
5	Families	170
6	Grounds	171
7	Initials	173
8	League Cricket	174
9	Minor Counties	175
10	Nicknames	176
11	Oddities	177
12	Two Sports	178
13	Unusual Dismissals	179
14	Odd One Out	180

15	Oxford V. Cambridge	182
16	Rest Of The World	182
17	Scratch Teams	183
18	Twelve To Find	184
19	Women's Cricket	185
20	Answers	187

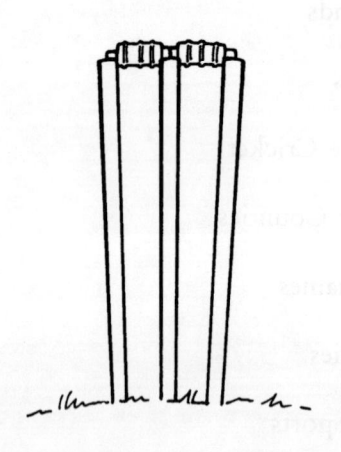

A MIXED BAG

A jumble of the interesting, innovative, unusual and downright curious.

ARISTOCRACY

Especially in the early days breeding was as important as batting.

1) When did the following head England Test sides?
   i) Lord Harris
   ii) Hon C.H. Tennyson

2) The Nawab of Pataudi Senior and Junior both skippered India but which other aristocrat led them against England in 1936?

3) Which ex-Northants player currently officiates as secretary to TCCB?

4) An England captain, later MCC President 1914-18. Name the noble lord?

5) His Highness the Jam Sehab of Nawanagar cut a dash for Sussex. How was he better known?

BODYLINE

Perhaps the most famous, or infamous series in cricket history.

1) What was the less emotive term for "bodyline" used by those who employed it?

2) Name England's three main strike bowlers.

3) Which county side did Jardine captain?

4) What was the result of the series?

5) Which Australian took 22 wickets in the series, a feat often overlooked?

COMMENTATORS

The men behind the "mike" are almost as fêted as those who play, indeed in some cases more so.

1) Who are
   i) "The Boil" ii) "A.R.L."
   iii) "The Alderman"?

2) At a Test you bumped into "Ollie" then held a conversation with "Blowers". Who did you encounter?

3) West Indies arrive on tour, who arrive in the Test match special box?

A Mixed Bag

4) Who takes humidity readings in an Aussie Test?

5) Which of the BBC team captained the 1970-71 Ashes winners?

6) Who doubled as commentator and wine correspondent for the *Guardian*?

7) Who is the doyen of Australian "mikemen"?

8) Which man in the box added a name by deed poll?

9) Who did A.R.L. replace as the BBC's frontman?

10) Who was the man in the hotseat when Sir Garfield Sobers launched his assault on Malcolm Nash?

11) Which Radio 3 man edits a major cricketing monthly?

12) Who is the "Head boy" and chief prankster on Radio 3?

13) Who once chaired the "Indoor League"?

14) In the BBC team who provides the pastel shades?

Cricket Quiz Book

15) "E.W." : Who do these famous initials apply to?

DOUBLE-BARRELLERS

Continuing the aristocratic theme...

1) Young cricketer of the year in 1972. Name him?

2) Conceded a remarkable 1-298 analysis in 1938. Who was he?

3) A forceful Derbyshire batsman of the 1970s?

4) Currently directing "Christians in Sport". Name the vicar?

5) Double-barrelled voiceover merchant who supports Surrey?

FAMILIES

Remarkable how in some families, class always shows through.

1) How many Hadlees have played Test cricket for New Zealand?

2) What are the Christian names of the three Amarnaths who have turned out for India?

A Mixed Bag

3) Which were the last pair of brothers to appear for England together?

4) Since 1973 New Zealand have fielded five sets of brothers in the same Test. Name them?

5) How many times did the Chappells — Ian and Greg — appear together?

6) Repeat the above question replacing Chappells with Pollocks.

7) Which country in the twentieth century fielded three brothers simultaneously?

8) What was unique about the appearance of G.G., A. and F.H. Hearne in the 1891-92 Test England v. South Africa?

9) Which father and son combinations played for different countries?

10) How many Tests respectively did J.H. and J.M. Parks play for England?

GROUNDS

1) Name the six domestic Test venues?

2) Where is the MCC based?

3) What is the West Indies' newest Test venue?

Cricket Quiz Book

4) Where is Gabba?

5) How many counties play at a "County Ground"?

6) Which ground hosted the 1987 World Cup Final?

7) Why did Glamorgan's Swansea stalwarts become annoyed in the 1988 close season?

8) How many days of County Championship cricket do the Yorkshire committee allocate to Kingston Upon Hull (before 1990)?

9) What's unusual about the Canterbury ground?

10) Which county plays at
    i) Moreton-in-the-marsh
    ii) Dudley
    iii) Wellingborough school
    iv) Worksop?

11) Which non-first-class ground boasts a two-day international festival?

12) Lancashire travel southwards for a Championship match at the Recreation ground. On Sunday they have a Refuge Assurance fixture at the County ground, Banister Park. Which two counties have they encountered?

A Mixed Bag

13) England on tour: a three-day game at Sabina Park followed by a Test at the Bourda Oval — which countries' customs stamps have the players collected?

14) Where are
    i) Eden Park and
    ii) Eden Gardens?

15) In the 1988 Test season which ground sprung a leak?

INITIALS

Always an integral part of the character of the game.

1) "W.W." — A speed merchant of much repute. Name him.

2) What were the initials of the Smiths who played for England in the 1960s?

3) The initials please of Mrs Knott's husband?

4) The initials of this Kent legend indicate a preference for one side of the wicket.

5) What were the initials of the "Brylcreem Boy"?

6) Bob the England skipper added a name to make what?

Cricket Quiz Book

7) C.J.P.G. belonged to a brief visitor to first-class cricket over here. Who?

8) Put in the initials of the Indian magicians:
   i) _____ Bedi
   ii) _____ Chandrasekher
   iii) _____ Prasana
   iv) _____ Venkataraghavan

9) Famous Australians:
   i) K.D. _____   iii) D.G. _____
   ii) R.B. _____

10) P.B.H. and E.R. former Test captains?

LEAGUE CRICKET

The lifeblood of the game in the north and home to so many top overseas stars.

1) When was the Lancashire league founded?

2) Who appeared in the Birmingham league and captained Australia post-Packer?

3) In 1986 Werneth unearthed a gem who quietly graduated to West Indies Test cricket. Name him?

4) The "Star" system dates from Nelson's signing of which cricketing legend in the 1920s?

A Mixed Bag

5) Two Sri Lankan Test players turned out in the 1986 Lancashire league. Name them.

6) Willie Watson, George Hirst and Wilfred Rhodes began their careers in which league?

7) For which Lancashire clubs did the following turn out?
   i) Charlie Griffith   iii) Winston Davis
   ii) Dennis Lillee

8) Which club is the odd one out? Crompton, Middleton, Rawtenstall, Rochdale and Royten

9) In which league did Bob Taylor, Len Higgs and Jack Ikin begin?

10) In the Bradford league this club is associated with the names of Hutton, Sutcliffe and Illingworth. Name it?

MINOR COUNTIES

Once-a-year visitors to the first-class stage in the NatWest, but their competition has a long and honourable history.

1) Which was the last first-class county to maintain a Second XI in the minors and who replaced them?

2) Who notched the title in 1980-81 and 1984?

3) Which famous cricketing family are associated with Norfolk?

4) In 1986 a ex-England batsman appeared in the top ten bowling averages. Name him?

5) Who were the last county Second XI to win the minor counties championship?

NICKNAMES

Part of the folklore of a game rich in characters.

1) Which legends acquired the following monikers?
    i) "The Croucher"
    ii) "The Demon"
    iii) "The Master"

2) West Indian pacemen attract flamboyant nicknames. Who are the following?
    i) "The big bird"
    ii) "Whispering death"
    iii) "Duracell"
    iv) "Diamond"

3) Two ironically named Test players attracted the epithet "Rowdy". Who were they?

A Mixed Bag

4) Which pace merchant rejoiced in the nickname "Typhoon"?

5) Which county pro's were known as the following?
   i) "The Dasher"
   ii) "The Demon from Frome"
   iii) "Professor"

6) In which Test side would you meet Zap, Lulu and Picca?

7) Which Test captains were
   i) "The Gnome"?
   ii) "Hubert"?

8) If "Smokey" bowled to "Paddles" with "Arkle" at the non-striker's end, who are the principles involved?

9) For whom did "Chilly" render yeoman service for many years?

10) Who was "Percy" — spinner of the 1970s?

ODDITIES

Some unusual incidents or people from the varied world of the game.

1) Which Test cricketer dazzled the crowd, but

Cricket Quiz Book

not the TCCB, by using a blue bat in a Sunday league match?

2) Which England Test star sports a Union Jack tattoo on one arm?

3) Glamorgan Player of the Year 1979 and Church Warden of St. Lukes Parish Church, Cardiff. Who was he?

4) Which star got into a thunderous argument over his metallic "willow"?

5) In pre-helmet days who batted in the 1975 World Cup Final under a blue sun hat?

TWO SPORTS

Less of them now in the demands of the modern game. These are multi-talented men whom we envy so much?

1) Fenced in the 1968 Olympics for Britain and spun for a southern county. Who is he?

2) Which soccer club did Denis and Leslie Compton and Arthur Milton join?

3) Which soccer clubs are the following most associated with?
   i) Jim Standen
   ii) Chris Balderstone
   ii) Ian Botham

A Mixed Bag

4) Who was the last English double internationalist in cricket and Rugby Union?

5) Which current county skipper has been an accomplished fullback for Lincoln City?

6) Three England Rugby Union internationals. Which county sides did they turn out for?
   i) Dusty Hare   iii) Alistair Hignell
   ii) Peter Squires

7) Eighteen Welsh Rugby Caps and a noted man of Glamorgan. Name him?

8) English soccer international, noted compiler of big scores and holder of the world long jump record. Who was this phenomenon?

9) Double Kiwi internationalist of the '70s and '80s in cricket and rugby. Name him?

10) Viv Richards has taken part in World Cups in two sports. Name his other love?

UNUSUAL DISMISSALS

Considering the number of ways to get out it is surprising batsmen ever made big scores.

1) What was odd about Matthew Maynard's exit in a 1988 Benson and Hedges final against Derbyshire?

Cricket Quiz Book

2) In 1951 Sir Len Hutton was given out against South Africa for a rare reason. Which one?

3) An odd manner of dismissal has been noted on the scorecard in a Test match for each of these players: Andrew Hilditch, Desmond Haynes, Mohsin Khan. How did they get out?

4) In 1969-70 run machine Zaheer Abbas' innings was abruptly curtailed in a manner which he has not yet repeated (playing for P.I.A. v. Karachi Blues). Why was he given out?

5) W. Huddlestone of Lancashire was bowled by R.D. Burrows of Worcestershire in 1911. Why does this incident still appear in the record books?

ODD ONE OUT

In each of the following sequences someone is the odd one out. (In each case it has nothing to do with whether the players are left- and right-handed.) Some are tongue-in-cheek.

1) Mervyn Kitchen, David Shephard, Colin Milburn, Harry Pilling.

2) Hedley Howarth, John Emburey, Ravi Shastri, Bishen Bedi.

A Mixed Bag

3) Erapalli Prosane, Bhagwant Chandrasekher, Maninder Singh, Inchan Ali, Sandeep Patil.

4) Lawrence Rowe, Gary Sobers, Frank Worrell, Malcolm Marshall, Wes Hall.

5) Eddie Barlow, Brian Davison, Graeme Pollock, Vincent Van Der Bijl.

6) Tony Nicholson, Chris Old, Johnny Wardle, Fred Trueman, Graeme Stevenson.

7) Canada, Bermuda, Holland, Denmark, Zimbabwe, Papua New Guinea.

8) Plunkett Shield, Currie Cup, Red Stripe Trophy, Ranfurly Shield, Quaid-E-Azam Trophy.

9) Greg Chappell, Gordon Greenidge, Frank Hayes, Doug Walters, Lawrence Rowe.

10) Kent, Essex, Somerset, Middlesex.

11) Intikhab Alam, Asif Masood, Abid Ali, Sayeed Ahmed, Younis Ahmed.

12) John Reid, Richard Collinge, Dick Motz, Greg Watson, John Parker.

13) Kerry O'Keefe, Jim Higgs, Ashley Mallett, Bob Holland, John Heeson.

Cricket Quiz Book

14) Denis Compton, Andy Sandham, John Edrich, Donald Bradman, Gary Sobers.

15) Majid Khan, Larry Gomes, Roy Fredericks, Javed Miandad, Collis King.

OXFORD V. CAMBRIDGE

The breeding ground where so many stars cut their teeth, with a history all of its own.

1) Since World War Two how many future England Captains scored tons in a varsity match?

2) What has been the highest team innings since the War?

3) What is the highest individual knock in a varsity match? Who scored it and when?

4) Other than M.J.K. Smith, who is the other player to have scored hundreds in three separate innings?

5) Who recorded 200 exactly in the 1970 varsity match?

REST OF THE WORLD

The special series that filled a gap in the Test schedules so admirably in 1970.

A Mixed Bag

1) What was the trophy that England and the Rest of the World played for in 1970?

2) How many South Africans took part in the series?

3) The following nations had one representative each. Name them.
   i) India   ii) Australia

4) What was the series result?

5) Which English participant was the only man from his side still active in the 1988 season?

SCRATCH TEAMS

It isn't all about the counties or Test sides. Part of cricket's charm is the number of historic teams which can still be found either in action or the record books.

1) Against which Invitation XI did Ken Rutherford pile up a mammoth 317 in 1986?

2) Only once did Sir Donald Bradman record a ton and a double-ton — in a match against Reyder's XI in 1929-30. Who was the Don playing for?

3) Gilbert Jessop constructed a 42-minute century against the Players of the South playing for which invitation outfit?

Cricket Quiz Book

4) Gordon Greenidge hit 13 sixes in 1974 for an Invitation XI normally associated with winter tours. Name the team.

5) The opening match of the English season is between the County Champions and which opponents?

TWELVE TO FIND

Something a little different. Some great sides are listed minus a couple of their stalwarts. Fill in the missing men.

<u>West Indies 1984</u>
Gordon Greenidge
Desmond Haynes
_____
Viv Richards
Clive Lloyd
Jeff Dujon
Malcolm Marshall
_____
Roger Harper
Michael Holding
Joel Garner

<u>Australia 1974-75</u>
Rick McCasker
Ian Redpath
Ian Chappell
Greg Chappell
_____
Doug Walters
Rodney Marsh
Max Walker
Jeff Thomson
Dennis Lillee

<u>Lancashire C 1971</u>

Farouk Engineer

<u>West Indies 1975 World Cup Final</u>

_____

A Mixed Bag

Barry Wood
_____
Clive Lloyd
Frank Hayes
John Sullivan
Jack Bond
David Hughes
Jack Simmons
Peter Lever
_____

Gordon Greenidge
Rohan Kanhai
Alvin Kallicharran
Clive Lloyd
Viv Richards
Derick Murray
Keith Boyce
Bernard Julien
Vanburn Holder
_____

England 1981
Geoff Boycott
Graham Gooch
David Gower
_____
Mike Gatting
Peter Willey
Ian Botham
John Emburey
Bob Taylor
_____
Bob Willis

Middlesex C 1984
Graeme Barlow
Wilf Slack
Clive Radley
Mike Gatting
_____
John Emburey
Phil Edmonds
Neil Williams
Norman Cowams
Wayne Daniel

WOMEN'S CRICKET

Perhaps we will be criticised for putting this in, or for not listing more questions.

1) Which playwright's daughter is a top female cricketer?

Cricket Quiz Book

2) What is the highest individual effort in a women's Test?

3) Played 25 times for England 1960-79, a record. Name her?

4) Who won the first women's world cup and when was it held?

5) When did the first England v. Australia Test take place?

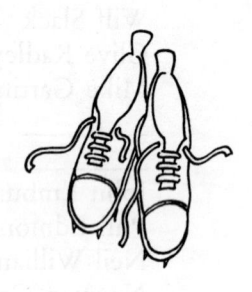

ANSWERS

ARISTOCRACY

1) i) 1878/9 and 1880-84   ii) 1921

2) The Maharajah of Vizianagram

3) Honourable Timothy Lamb

4) Lord Hawke

5) K.S. Ranjitsinhji

BODYLINE

1) Leg theory

2) Harold Larwood, Bill Bowes and Bill Voce

3) Surrey

4) 4-1 in England's favour

5) Bill O'Reilly

Cricket Quiz Book

COMMENTATORS

1) i) Trevor Bailey ii) Tony Lewis
   iii) Don Mosey

2) Colin Millburn and Henry Blofeld

3) Tony Cosier

4) Tony Grieg

5) Ray Illingworth

6) John Arlott

7) Alan McGillivray

8) Bob Willis — "R.G.D." "D" for Dylan

9) Peter West

10) Wilf Wooller

11) Christopher Martin-Jenkins

12) Brian Johnston

13) Fred Trueman

14) Richie Benaud (and suits)!

15) E.W. "Jim" Swanton

Answers

DOUBLE-BARRELLERS

1) Dudley Owen-Thomas (Surrey)

2) Laurie Fleetwood-Smith

3) Ashley Harvey-Walker

4) Andrew Wingfield-Digby

5) Christopher Martin-Jenkins

FAMILIES

1) Three: Richard, Dale and father Walter (Barry played in the World Cup only.)

2) Lalla, Mohinder, Surinder

3) P.E. and D. W. Richardson (1957)

4) Hadlee — Dale and Richard, Crowe — Geoff and Martin, Howarth — Geoff and Hedley, Parker — John and Jeff, Bracewell — John and Brendan

5) 43 times

6) 23 times

7) Pakistan — the Mohammeds

Cricket Quiz Book

8) A. and G.G. played for England, the third brother for South Africa

9) M. Jehangir Khan (India) and Majid Khan (Pakistan), Nazar Mohammed (India) and Mudassar Nazar (Pakistan), S. Wazir Ali (India) and Khalid Wazir (Pakistan)

10) J.H. (1), J.M. (46)

GROUNDS

1) Edgbaston, Trent Bridge, Headingley, Old Trafford, The Oval and Lord's

2) Lord's

3) St Johns Antigua

4) Brisbane

5) Ten

6) Wankhede Stadium, Bombay

7) Because of the threat to hold more 3/4-day championship games at Sophia Gardens, Cardiff.

8) None

9) The oak tree on the playing surface.

Answers

10) i) Gloucestershire
    ii) Worcestershire
    iii) Northants
    iv) Notts

11) Jesmond

12) Somerset and Hampshire

13) Jamaica and Guyana

14) i) Auckland   ii) Calcutta

15) Headingley

INITIALS

1) Wes Hall (West Indies)

2) M.J.K. and A.C.

3) A.F.E. — Alan Knott

4) Les (L.E.G.) Ames

5) D.C.S. (Denis) Compton

6) R.G.D. Willis

7) C.J.P.G. Van Zyl

Cricket Quiz Book

8) i) B.S. ii) B.S.
   iii) E.A.S. iv) S.

9) i) Walters ii) Simpson
   iii) Bradman

10) P.B.H. May and E.R. "Ted" Dexter

LEAGUE CRICKET

1) 1890

2) Graham Yallop

3) Carl Hooper

4) Sir Learie Constantine

5) Ravi Ratnayeke and A.L.F. De Mel

6) Huddersfield and District

7) i) Burnley ii) Haslingden
   iii) Rishton

8) Rawtenstall — it is Lancs League, the others are Central Lancs.

9) Staffordshire

10) Pudsey St Lawrence

Answers

MINOR COUNTIES

1) Somerset — replaced by Wales 1988

2) Durham

3) The Edrich family

4) Graham Roope (Berkshire)

5) Yorkshire II 1971

NICKNAMES

1) i) Gilbert Jessop ii) F.E. Spofforth
   iii) Sir Jack Hobbs

2) i) Joel Garner
   ii) Michael Holding
   iii) Courtney Walsh
   iv) Wayne Daniel

3) Chris Tavare and Ashley Mallett

4) Frank Tyson

5) i) Peter Denning ii) Chris Dredge
   iii) Peter Roebuck

6) England, Graham Gooch, David Gower and Graham Dilley

Cricket Quiz Book

7) i) Keith Fletcher   ii) Clive Lloyd

8) Norman Featherstone to Richard Hadlee with Derek Randall watching.

9) Yorkshire — Chris Old

10) Pat Pocock

ODDITIES

1) Graham Roope

2) Bill Athey

3) Tony Cordle

4) Dennis Lillee

5) Gordon Greenidge

TWO SPORTS

1) David Acfield (Essex)

2) Arsenal

3) i) West Ham
   ii) Scunthorpe United
   iii) Carlisle

Answers

4) M.J.K. Smith

5) Phil Neale (Worcestershire)

6) i) Nottinghamshire
   ii) Yorkshire
   iii) Gloucestershire

7) Wilf Wooller

8) C.B. Fry

9) Brian Mckechnie

10) Soccer

UNUSUAL DISMISSALS

1) Helmet fell on wicket.

2) Obstructing the field.

3) Handling the ball. Hilditch v. Pakistan 1978-79

4) Hitting the ball twice.

5) The bail travelled a record 67 yards 6 inches.

ODD ONE OUT

1) Harry Pilling is a small man amongst rotund companions.

2) John Embury is the only off spinner.

3) Inchan Ali is a West Indian among Indians.

4) Lawrence Rowe is a Jamaican among Barbadians.

5) Brian Davison is a Rhodesian among South Africans.

6) Tony Nicholson was not capped for his country.

7) Papua New Guinea was never in an ICC Final.

8) Ranfurly Shield is a rugby trophy.

9) Gordon Greenidge was not a Test debutant centurion.

10) Somerset have never managed to win the County Championship.

11) Abid Ali is an Indian Among Pakistanis.

12) Greg Watson is an Aussie among Kiwis.

Answers

13) Ashley Mallett is an off spinner among leg spinners.

14) Denis Compton never notched a Test triple hundred.

15) Larry Gomes was never a Glamorgan player.

OXFORD V. CAMBRIDGE

1) Four: M.J.K. Smith 1954-55-56, M. Cowdrey 1953, A. Lewis 1962, J. M. Brearley 1962-64. Note: Derek Pringle captained England in the field in 1988 — a centurion in 1979.

2) 457 (Oxford) 1947

3) Nawab of Pataudi Senior 238 not out for Oxford

4) Robin Boyd-Moss 1982 and twice in 1983

5) Majid Khan

REST OF THE WORLD

1) The Guiness Trophy

2) Five: Eddie Barlow, Mike Proctor, Barry Richards, Peter and Graeme Pollock

Cricket Quiz Book

3) i) Farouk Engineer
   ii) Graham Mackenzie

4) 4-1 to the rest

5) Keith Fletcher

SCRATCH TEAMS

1) Brian Close's XI Scarborough 1986

2) Woodfull's XI

3) Gentlemen of the South 191 (1907)

4) D.H. Robin's XI

5) MCC

TWELVE TO FIND

Larry Gomes — Eldine Baptise

Ross Edwards — Ashley Mallett

Harry Pilling — Ken Shuttleworth

Roy Fredericks — Andy Roberts

Answers

Mike Brearley — Graham Dilley/Chris Old

Roland Butcher — Paul Downton

WOMEN'S CRICKET

1) Dennis Potter (Sarah)

2) 190, Sandiya Aggarwal, July 1986

3) Rachel Hayhoe-Flint

4) England 1973

5) 1934